HOUSE HACKING 101

HOW TO LIVE FOR FREE

Purchasing, Financing, and Managing By-The-Room
Rental Houses (Without Losing Your Mind)

AUTOMATED RETIREES

© Copyright 2021 - All rights reserved.

The content contained within this book may not be reproduced, duplicated, or transmitted without direct written permission from the author or the publisher.

Under no circumstances will any blame or legal responsibility be held against the publisher, or author, for any damages, reparation, or monetary loss due to the information contained within this book, either directly or indirectly.

Legal Notice:

This book is copyright protected. It is only for personal use. You cannot amend, distribute, sell, use, quote, or paraphrase any part, or the content within this book, without the consent of the author or publisher.

Disclaimer Notice:

Please note the information contained within this document is for educational and entertainment purposes only. All effort has been executed to present accurate, up-to-date, reliable, complete information. No warranties of any kind are declared or implied. Readers acknowledge that the author is not engaged in the rendering of legal, financial, medical, or professional advice. The content within this book has been derived from various sources. Please consult a licensed professional before attempting any techniques outlined in this book.

By reading this document, the reader agrees that under no circumstances is the author responsible for any losses, direct or indirect, that are incurred due to the use of the information contained within this document, including, but not limited to, errors, omissions, or inaccuracies.

CONTENTS

Part 1: The Introduction 1

    Introduction 2

    Chapter 1: Why House Hacking Is the PERFECT First Stream of Passive Income 10

    Chapter 2: Goals, Taxes, and Lenders, Oh My! 29

Part 2: Buying Your House Hacking Heaven and Finding Angels for Tenants 56

    Chapter 3: Purchasing a New House 57

    Chapter 4: The Zero Stress Tenant Vetting System 82

Part 3: Living Large and In Charge 127

    Chapter 5: How to Live With Tenants—Peacefully 128

    Conclusion 153

    References 157

Part 1

The Introduction

Introduction

Being rich is having money; being wealthy is having time.

~ Margaret Bonnano

Living for free is one goal that almost every human shares. No one likes work, especially not at a job that slowly sucks your soul out of your eyeballs!

Everyone wants it, but so few people know how to get it. If you tell anyone that you want to live for free, retire at 30, or do anything else out of the ordinary, they tell you that you can't.

It simply isn't done! They say while sipping their tea and looking longingly out of their window. *You must work until you're 69-½.*

Well, excuse me, but who in their right mind wants to do that?

I used to live in New Orleans. If you ever go there, you must visit St. Charles Cathedral. It's gigantic and beautiful, almost eerie in how close you feel to God when you walk through its doors - even if you don't believe in him.

I don't know the specifics, but about 200 years ago, someone decided to build that Cathedral; I'm not sure why, how, or who, but they did. And it took a gargantuan effort to organize, pay for, and finally build it.

Hundreds of laborers had to work on that thing, if not *thousands*. And it truly is a beauty that has survived the test of time. Several wars and terrible hurricanes later, it's still there . . .making its mark on humanity.

And when you walk through those doors, you get such an eerie sense of calm; it almost makes you want to cry. Someone built that. They thought of it, planned it, and made it happen. And it's beautiful, there for all to see.

If someone can do that, surely I can figure out how to live for free.

It can't be as hard as building an entire, eerie cathedral! It certainly isn't as challenging as building the Egyptian pyramids millennia ago! Humans are amazing creatures with minds with the capacity to do great things.

So, why can't you figure out how to live for free?

I wrote this book for a variety of reasons. First, too many people are told they can't do something when, actually, *they can*. It's a simple statement. *You can't do that* is a prevalent phrase where I'm from. *You simply can't*!

Ignore that person. Even if that person is you.

Living for free is much easier than it sounds. First, you have to have a place to live. (I hope you do - even if you're renting.) Once you have a place to live, you need to figure out how to rent or sublet out portions of it.

Do you know of the concept of *arbitrage?*

Arbitrage is buying a lot of something and then selling it piece by piece.

Like Walmart. They buy millions of *a thing* from China, Mexico, or even the United States. Since they're buying a million, they get it at a vast discount. Then they sell it, piece by piece, to you because you can't buy a million of something to get that discount!

You can do this with a house. You buy - or rent - the entire house and then rent out the rooms, room by room, to people who don't want to buy one or don't think they can. Since you're renting it out by the room, you charge a bit of a premium. Maybe the per-room rate in your town is $750, and a house payment is $1500. Rent out two rooms, and you technically get to live for free.

It's so simple that people have been doing it for hundreds of years!

The first hurdle you must jump over is owning a house. You're either going to need to buy one or rent one. For some, this might involve moving to an area with a lower cost of living, temporary-but-extreme budgeting, or taking a second job.

None of those things are easy, but they are *doable*. Remember, you're part of the same species of beings that built the pyramids. Did that seem *reasonable* to you? Does that sound *easy?*

Then, once you have a down payment, you buy a house. It doesn't matter if you can afford to pay the monthly payments on this house; all that matters is that you can charge your tenants enough to pay for the house. We'll go over that in detail later on in the book.

Once you've found a house you know you can pay for with other people's money, you can focus on finding people you will enjoy living with. That's definitely easier said than done! Still, there are a few tricks to make sure you do it right and find people you can stand.

That's about it! I've been house hacking for the better part of 10 years. While it is not as fun as living alone, it is 100% worth it. If you've read any of my other books, you know that I am trying to retire early. I'm 26, and I want to retire by the time I'm 30. That's not easy, but it's sure easier than building a spaceship that can take three astronauts to the moon!

House hacking was the beginning of that journey for me. And it's 100% doable, even if you're too poor to afford your own house right now. You can own a property! And I will show you how.

How to Get The Most Out of This Book

To help you along your House Hacking journey, we've created a free Done For You bonus companion course that includes spreadsheets, templates, and additional resources.

We highly recommend you sign up now to get the most out of this book. You can do that by going to the link below.

www.AutomatedRetirees.com/HouseHacking

Free Bonus #1: House Hacking Profitability Calculator ($97 value)

This spreadsheet will help you very quickly determine if a house you are looking at is profitable. The tactics you learn in this book pair perfectly with this calculator to ensure you never buy a bad deal.

Free Bonus #2: The Peace Keeper's Rulebook ($19 value)

A happy house is a peaceful house. In my experience, the best way to make your house peaceful is for everyone to agree to a set of rules. This rulebook template has some basic rules I've found to keep the peace. And it is editable so if you have a special circumstance, you can also add your own!

Free Bonus #3: Perfect Realtor Interview Questions ($19 value)

Do you have a realtor? If not, you'll need to find one! Just like any other profession, there are good realtors, bad realtors, and GREAT realtors! I've put together a realtor interview that will help you hire a great ones so you can find the perfect house in no time flat!

Free Bonus #4: The Definitive List of Shared Items for House Hacking ($29 value)

If you're worried about setting your house up for success, then this is exactly what you need. It goes over everything from what furniture your tenants will expect (and where to buy it) to the consumables you'll need to provide. Start your House Hacking off on the right foot!

Free Bonus #5: House Hacking Room Profitability Tracker ($19 value)

The first step to comping an investment is to figure out how much monthly profit it will bring in. With House Hacking, we make money by renting out our rooms. This must-have spreadsheet helps you determine what rooms are worth in your area, ensuring you invest in a profitable home.

All of these bonuses are 100% free, with no strings attached. You don't need to provide any personal details except your first name and email address.

To get your bonuses, go to:

www.AutomatedRetirees.com/HouseHacking

CHAPTER 1

Why House Hacking Is the PERFECT First Stream of Passive Income

Landlords grow rich in their sleep without working, risking, or economizing.

~ John Stuart Mill

What You Can Expect From This Chapter

- *The who, what, where, when, and why of house hacking*
- *How to find the best house to hack (or maximize your current space)*

To Hack or Not To Hack - That Is The Question

How often do you flip through interior design magazines and see the beautiful LA mansions of the rich and famous? Beyond that, if you've seen reality TV shows like *Million Dollar Listing*, you'll know that California is filled with modern luxury homes that sell for the same price as a small island.

California is full of expensive real estate. In some cities, a three-bedroom/two-bath home built in the '60s can sell for three million. House hacking is the perfect strategy for Californians. Even if you make an above-average salary, you must work several years to have enough for a down payment.

House hacking is quite common in many affluent areas (especially in the tech hubs) or suburbs with big homes. Big cities are also seeing a massive spike in house hacking – mainly in cities where the housing costs have shot through the roof!

The Ins and Outs of House Hacking

House hacking is an old concept with a new name. It's likely been around for as long as houses have existed. My family passes down a lot of wisdom through stories, and quite a few involve tales of the various house-boarders my grandparents and great grandparents had back in the 1930s.

How to Live for Free

My family traveled to the United States from Italy back in the '20s. Like most immigrants in that time, they were poor, owning pretty much nothing except for the clothes on their backs. My great-grandparents worked hard for almost nothing, so they learned to be crafty with their money.

Renting out rooms is one surefire way to turn almost nothing into something. They worked their way up to owning a small, two-bedroom house – one bed for the kids, one for the parents.

Their neighborhood was a very tight-knit community. My family specialized in laying bricks, plumbing, and woodworking. They, along with other neighbors, would take turns building rooms on each other's homes.

When my family finally got an extra room, they decided they would rent it. After all, the kids were doing fine in their room, and it was a great way to make a little extra money. I mean, they had five kids! *Do you know how much kids eat?!*

And now, here I am, almost 100 years later, renting out my house too. Everyone needs a place to live and if you have some unused space, renting it is as close to making something out of nothing that you'll ever get.

I'm fortunate because only two of the four extra bedrooms in my home are rented out. I used to rent out *every extra room* I could, but I've learned to use the extra money from my house to set up other passive or semi-passive income streams. So, I'm afforded the luxury of two vacant rooms; one serves as my office and the other as a guest bedroom. This is the beginning of my wealthy life!

But what if I lived in California? There's a full-on housing crisis there. If you want to live within 90 minutes of a big city, you will pay a high price. I learned this the hard way when I flew out to Mountain View for a job interview.

I had the pleasure (and it was a *pleasure*!) of staying in Sunnyvale, a quiet little town with a bustling downtown area. Every day, I'd take a nice little walk from my hotel to a different coffee shop. Despite it being the middle of December, the weather was beautiful, and the quaint little '60s houses with gigantic fruit trees were a special treat to walk through.

Like any great real estate investor, I had to check out some of these houses' prices. I knew they'd be out of my price range because, admittedly, I like to invest in cheap properties . . . but HOLY COW! A 2-bedroom, 2-bath house on a tiny lot was selling for 2.8 million. *And* it was outdated!

I bought this same house last year for $80,000... I couldn't help but put my phone away and stare off in the distance, disturbed.

That's why the house hacking scene in California is the way it is. People pay $1500 to live *on a platform for the switchback stairs.* Or in a walk-in closet. You have five people in a two-bedroom house! It's nuts. And bigger houses just make up for it by having more tenants.

House hacking is the usual approach when you can't afford where you're living; it's infinitely better to rent out a room than work a second job. And the people who rent these rooms love it because they get a cheap place to live. It's a win-win for everyone involved!

By far, the best way to house hack is purchasing a duplex, triplex, or fourplex and renting out the units you don't use. If you stay there, this separates you from your tenant while also generating cash flow.

However, if you can't get one because they are too expensive in your area or you already own a house, then I have a few tricks up my sleeve for you. I'll talk about these strategies at length later on.

House hacking - done the right way - allows the investor to live in their property for free—making the investment worth more than every penny!

To live for free, the house you need to buy depends on these three things . . .

- How much your mortgage is
- How many rooms or spaces you have to rent
- How much you can charge for rent

. . . and *these* heavily depend on your location. After all, what you pay for a tiny house in Cali buys you a *mansion* in Florida.

Another great benefit: some of the shared expenses (think electricity, Wi-Fi, water bill) are split between each person living in the house, bringing the cost down even further!***

***If you look at your electricity and water bill, you'll see that a substantial portion of it is the delivery fee! There are also things you use in your house that run often or continuously; the fridge, ac/heat, sprinklers - those use water and electricity too. So, even though the bill will be slightly higher with others living there, you'll still pay less when you split it.

House Hacking for First-Time Home Buyers

The house hacking model works particularly well for first-time home buyers and military veterans. These two groups receive many loan benefits like better interest rates, lower down payments, and other helpful government programs.

When most people start in the real estate industry, they have little money to play around with or spend upfront. Usually, they only have enough for a down payment and carrying out minor renovations. If you make your first investment in your own house, you get to learn how to buy a house, how to deal with tenants, *and* you get a free place to live. Plus, you garner the benefits of being a first-time homebuyer.

I started house hacking in college. Back then, I sublet a few rooms in the apartments where I lived. When I left college, I continued to sublet until I had enough money for a house. I've hacked with strangers, family, and friends.

You might think that family is the best type of person to live with, but strangers have benefits too. At least you can kick them out without making your mom cry!

Just kidding; I've never made my mom cry.

Family, friends, strangers – it doesn't matter who you live with. Every story is the same. You need to set rules, and you need to make sure they don't trash your property. That can be harder with family than strangers because they might try to use their status as your brother to justify scratching your floor.

Being a bit of a control freak, this has been a great personal journey for me; I transformed from a militant drill sergeant into a people-manager, learning to resolve problems without ruffling a lot of feathers. Especially my own.

In terms of solving those problems, house hacking is great; you're right there, in the middle of all the action, monitoring the cleanliness and upkeep of your house every day. So, instead of waiting six months, you can have that out-of-body, deeply-disturbing anger *immediately* after your brother-in-law accidentally pulls the towel rack off the wall. And that can be the difference between just a bad day and a moldy wall.

In short, it's easier for you to address your tenants' concerns and carry out maintenance on the property before minor problems become major ones. Even though you live with others, if you set the proper rules and boundaries, you can even be happy while you do it.

So, what should first-time buyers know about house hacking before they start their journey? First, you need to ensure that you purchase a property appropriate for house hacking. Some general criteria:

- House with several bedrooms and bathrooms (it would be a bonus if it also had more than one entry point)
- House in a desirable location (jobs, places to shop, and stuff to do nearby)
- House with feasible costs when compared to local rent (this would put less strain on you and ensure that your rent isn't ghastly-high)

- House that looks aesthetically pleasing (no professional wants to feel like they are living in a dorm)

A bit later, we'll consider if your house is, indeed, a perfect house for hacking. For now, let's start with some strategies.

What Are the Different House Hacking Strategies?

Regardless of which house hacking strategy you use, you will pursue one goal: Covering your mortgage with the generated rent monies. When I say *mortgage*, it's in a nebulous way; maybe your "rent" is college savings, a better car, or saying goodbye to your second job. In this book, "covering your mortgage" substitutes for any goal you use your property to reach.

If you have the luxury of buying a house, then bigger is almost always better. They have more rooms and generally aren't much more expensive than smaller houses in the same neighborhood.

My husband and I broke the number one rule when purchasing a house: *never buy the biggest house in the neighborhood.* I'm not sure who coined this phrase or why it's even a rule, but – at least technically – your house with be worth less per square foot if you ever sell it, but *who says I'll ever sell this house?*

My house is a monstrous five-bedroom/three-bath with two living areas and a dining room I proudly converted to a gym. (Pics at the end if you want to see it!)

My neighbors, who bought a three-bedroom/two-bath with one living room and no dining room, paid just $30,000 less than us. It didn't help that they bought their house six months later in one of the most significant appreciation periods that Austin has ever seen. However, even if they'd bought at the same time, it still would have been about $45,000 less.

And it's not like we only paid $100,000 for the house; we paid around $275,000.

The general rule of thumb is, each $10,000 adds an extra $100 to the monthly mortgage. So, by paying $30,000 more, we added $300 to our monthly mortgage – but we also have two more rooms to rent out. The going rate for rent in my area is $700 for a room with access to a hallway bathroom. If you rent out just one room . . ..well, you get the point.

So, let's go over some of the different strategies people commonly use when they house hack.

1. Multi-Family Properties

We already briefly discussed this strategy; any 2+-unit building is a terrific property for house hacking. The more units, the more cost-effective it will be. Further, fourplexes are usually not four times more expensive than single-family homes, even though they are technically four houses in one. While your mortgage payment will be more, you'll have a higher cash flow by renting three units instead of just one - assuming that you're living in one of the fourplex units.

Banks also consider four-plexes as *residential property*, allowing you to get a standard residential loan for them. However, anything above that requires a commercial loan.

Duplexes, triplexes, and fourplexes are very popular for house hacking because they are cost-effective. Plus, you can retain your own living space within them; you'll just share a wall with your tenant.

2. Finished Basements

Do you live somewhere where basements exist? Then you can spruce yours up and turn yours into another house! You can even fit it with its en-suite, kitchen, living room, and entry/exit point.

To be as cost-effective as possible, you could live in your basement and rent out the house are above. Even if you rent the house out by the room, you will have your own space away from everyone else. You could also fit your basement, so it has two rooms leading to a kitchen area.

We rarely have basements in Texas because they're so expensive to build here. You'd have to almost literally blow up the bedrock that sits just under a thin layer of dirt. *(It's for the best, though, because my husband's dream is to have a secret, underground lair. Even if we did have one, I doubt we'd get to use it for house hacking!)*

3. Additional Dwelling Units (ADU)

Additional Dwelling Units are external buildings not connected to the main structure on a property. They are usually in the backyard.

Think of a self-sufficient cottage you build for your grandparents or in-laws to live in when they come to visit. These units are fitted with the necessary plumbing and electrical structures to make it a safe and livable home.

If you have one of these units (or have acquired permits to build one), you can use it for house hacking. What's great with having an ADU is that while you and your tenants live on the same property, you have your own separate living spaces. Heck, you have your own separate house!

Some people are purchasing "tiny homes" and putting them in their backyard. When I looked into doing this, I faced two problems. First, my HOA doesn't allow it. Second, tiny homes are expensive! It might make sense for you and your situation if you already own a house, have the money for a down payment on a tiny home, and would like to keep your own space.

I like to peruse www.tinyhouselistings.com occasionally to see what's trending. I am considering building a tiny house park. But that's a conversation for another book!

4. Houses With Multiple Bedrooms

If you can't afford a multifamily home, then the next best thing is a big single-family home. To cover your mortgage and still have enough left to live on, you need to purchase *as big a house as your down payment can support*. It doesn't matter how big the backyard is or if the bedrooms all have their private bathroom – you just need a lot of rooms. It's best if you have one bathroom for every two rental areas.

When searching for a single-family home, focus on finding one within your price range with as many bedrooms as possible. If you have the option to purchase a big, outdated house over a smaller, newer home, choose the big, old house. A couple of grand can go a long way towards repainting the walls and refurbishing the floors. As long as it has good bones, go for it!

Professionals and other desirable tenants will be attracted to houses that are cute, decorated, and clean. This goes beyond charging more for rent - you want your house to look good because you want to attract good tenants. Without good tenants, house hacking will not work. At least, it won't work *well*.

If you know that you are not going to work on fixing up an old house (or you don't have the money to), it's best to go with a smaller, more well-kept home. Whatever you choose, do the math to make sure what buy helps you reach your goal. Have an honest conversation with yourself if you are planning on flipping an older house; you need to flip it, and you need to *flip it fast*.

Mine is a five-bedroom house. My tenants have their rooms and a living room upstairs, while Eddy and I have our bedroom and living room downstairs. It works well for us because we all have our private sections of the house. We rarely see each other, and everyone respects everyone else's space. This is normally how it works, no matter who you're rooming with.

5. DIY: Building More Rooms

If you cannot find (or afford) property with a lot of bedrooms, cheat a little by making a living room, open office area, or dining room into a bedroom. You must do a little extra work, but it will be worth it in the end for an extra month's rent.

Typically, a house hacker will opt to sleep in their living room, renting the master bedroom out. The master bedrooms fetch a lot more on the rental market because they're larger than normal bedrooms and usually have a private, luxurious bathroom. In my market, master bedrooms can be up to $300 extra per month!

If you choose to live in your living room, bamboo room dividers are a cheap way to give yourself privacy. Just make sure you have access to a toilet and a shower, and you should be ok. It's not optimal for three people to share a bathroom, but it works.

When I graduated from college, we house hacked a tiny two-bedroom/one-bath apartment to pay off our debt. Is sharing a bathroom with a guy who sheds more hair than a husky something I relished? No, but the inconvenience was worth it to pay off that expensive student loan bill!

You might have to make some sacrifices when you house hack – but they are worth it. Just like anything else, you need to be crafty to jump ahead of the pack. And if you need the money or want to retire early, then these small inconveniences are worth it. *(And some can even be fixed by a cheap Roomba.)*

Is House Hacking the Best Model for Me?

The best thing about entering the real estate industry is there are multiple ways of generating wealth, catering to different investors with different lifestyles and personalities. Although I'm a fan of house hacking, I know that it's not everyone's first pick. Below are a few points that will help you determine if house hacking might be worthwhile for you.

- You want to retire early
- You have a house or a space you don't mind renting for some extra income
- You don't have a house, but you still want some extra income
- You don't have a huge appetite for risk, but you want to make extra income
- You don't mind interacting with your tenants occasionally
- You want a little more practice being a landlord before you purchase an investment property

- You want to purchase a home; however, you live in an expensive area or are just very budget-minded
- You are always traveling or moving around a lot for work
- You want to invest in real estate but have very little money
- You are barely staying afloat and could really use a little extra income

If you have identified with any of the above points, then you are the perfect candidate for house hacking. Just to add a cherry on top, here are a few benefits you can look forward to with house hacking:

- You can literally live for free if you follow the instructions in this book. If you already own a house, you can significantly reduce your housing expenses.
- It's a great entry point into being a landlord because you get to live with your tenants and monitor their treatment of your investment.
- It's a great passive income generator!
- House hacking uses residential housing—an asset that almost always appreciates.

- It's very low risk because you already have the most important part: the property! If you want a *house hacking trial run*, you can also try medium or short-term renting, like Airbnb.

- Renting out rooms in your home is also a solid strategy for wealth generation. Rich people become rich because they make money while they sleep. This represents an excellent first step for you on your path to true wealth!

TL;DR

(Too long, didn't read. A summary of each chapter for those of you who like to 3x your YouTube videos!)

To successfully carry out this model, you must live in an area where other people want or need to live. Cities and suburbs work great for long-term house hacking. Rural areas are a little more challenging but may work better for short-term rentals. Like Airbnb! (people LOVE to get away!)

This investment is a tradeoff between comfort and money. Eddy (my husband) and I choose not to rent out over two rooms in our home because that's what we are comfortable with.

How to Live for Free

Nothing stops us from renting out over two rooms; I have some friends who rent out three rooms plus an open office space! All said and done, the number of rooms you rent is up to you, your wallet, and your personal comfort level!

CHAPTER 2

Goals, Taxes, and Lenders, Oh My!

Don't wait for opportunity; create it!

~ Unknown

What You Can Expect From This Chapter

- *The importance of creating and achieving your house hacking goals*
- *How to find, talk to, and convince lenders to lend to you*
- *A new homeowner's guide to taxes*

What Makes a Business a Business?

In 2005, my parents' friends, Mr. and Mrs. T, bought a five-bedroom house. They had two kids and wanted an office space and a guest bedroom. Eventually, their kids grew up and moved out, leaving them with four bedrooms, two bathrooms, and an entire game room of unused space! It was upstairs, neatly tucked out of the way, so most of the time, they didn't even think about those rooms. But they sure did pay for them!

At church one day, their pastor informed the congregation he knew someone who had fallen on hard times. Mr. and Mrs. T offered to put them up for a while in one of their unused rooms. *We're not using them, so why not help someone?*

After about six months, their guest finally had their life back together and moved out. But not before leaving Mr. and Mrs. T a gift: $1000! While it certainly didn't cover six months of rent, they hadn't expected anything in return, so they were delighted and very thankful.

At the time, both of their kids had moved on to college – challenging enough for anyone to pay for nowadays – but Mr. and Mrs. T didn't have very lucrative careers. They were part of middle America that makes too little to pay for college but too much to qualify for scholarships. They had been surviving, but it had been hard.

But, after that surprise *than- you* money from their church friend, something clicked.

They could rent their rooms out for money!

They decided that they didn't mind having one guest, so . . . maybe they'd try two. After all, they did have two extra bedrooms now. They put a futon in the office so their kids would have a room if they came home for the summer and fixed up those extra rooms for long-term renters.

Mr. and Mrs. T live in a big tech city, so renting their rooms worked out great. They found two young professionals who wanted to sign a year-long lease and pay $600 per month. One had a dog, so he had to pay $150 extra.

Now they made an extra $1350. That isn't chump change; it represented a $16,000 raise!

That's life-changing money!

While it didn't cover it all, the rent income immensely helped pay off their kids' tuition.

And you know what? They rarely had terrible experiences with their tenants because they did due diligence beforehand. It took a little longer, but they found people with similar values and levels of cleanliness. They also relied on a shared set of rules from the beginning – avoiding disputes and allowing them to all live in harmony.

Even now, after both of their boys finished college and moved on, Mr. and Mrs. T still rent out two rooms. But all that money now goes towards their retirement!

When you stop to think about it, they got a raise for doing about an hour's worth of work each week. It helped them pay for college for not just one – but *two* kids. And it wasn't even hard! As you can see, they already had the space, but even if you don't, it's still not that complicated.

But it all starts with figuring out your goals.

Let's Get Down To Business

So, why do this? What's your reason for going through all the trouble of finding a space in your house (or even buying a new house), renting it, and dealing with a tenant? In the real estate investing biz, we call this *your why*.

Like Mr. and Mrs. T, some people want to save up some extra money because they have a significant expense. Some want some help with their bills or – yes – to even live for free! Others do this to generate some passive income they can throw into other investments.

Whatever your *why*, it will have a monetary aspect. To live for free, how much is your mortgage? If you have a huge expense coming up, how much is *that* going to cost? For investing, how many houses do you want to invest in each year, and what would you like to pay as a down payment?

I find it easier to break these monetary goals into a span of months; after all, you'll be making monthly income from house hacking.

If you're just trying to live for free, you already know the number (or you will shortly if you don't have a house!) It's the price of your mortgage plus utilities.

If you're saving for a big expense, like college, figure out how many months you have until you need to pay for it and divide the expense by that number. If college is $10,000 per semester and you take two semesters per year, you'll need $20,000 for one year. $20,000 / 12 is equal to $1540 per month.

Investing is similar to paying for a significant expense. You'll need the down payment plus a nest egg. I recommend at least 10% down plus $5,000 per investment property. Once you know how many houses you'd like to invest in and how expensive they are, you can determine how much you want to save up.

Let's say you want to invest in two houses next year and each cost $80,000. You'll pay a 10% down payment for each, allowing another 2% for closing costs. So, your total financial goal is 12% of $160,000 – plus $5,000 a piece for renovations: $29,200. Dividing that by 12 (to account for months), you need to save $2,434 per month. If you rent out four rooms a month, that's just $600 per room.

So, what's your goal?

Grab a post-it note or a notebook and write it down where you can see it. This is an old trick that real estate investors use to help us remember our *why*. Every time you feel pain, you can look at that post-it note and remember why you are doing what you're doing.

But, knowing what you want to make each year is only half the battle. We also need to figure out:

- How much house you can buy
- What each room can be rented for *in your area*

If you already own a home and are not looking to purchase another one, you can skip to the next section because this chapter is all about the first point: how much house can you buy? Only one entity can decide that: a lender. If you're ready to buy a house, this next section is all for you!

I Got The Money, Honey!

I have never even set foot in a house, let alone looked for my perfect property. I've heard of "lenders" before, but I don't even know what they do. Why would I need to talk to a lender now? Ah!

Whenever you want to buy a new property, the first step is always talking to someone who lends money.

Banks and credit unions will eventually lend you money for a house. The amount of money they are willing to lend you depends on a few different factors they have condensed to *an affordability score*, a measure based on your credit score and total income.

The general rule of thumb is you can only afford a house worth three times your yearly salary. If you and your partner (a co-signer) make $100,000 per year together, lenders will generally lend up to $300,000. This number also depends heavily on the interest rate. A 3% interest rate will get you a lot more house for the same monthly payment than a 5% interest rate.

The easiest way to figure out what they will lend you is to *talk to them*. Sometimes, there's logic to what they are doing, and other times, they seemingly just pull a number out of a hat. It's logical to do this before you even step foot in a potential purchase because if you don't know how much they will lend, you don't know how much you can spend.

If you've had some credit troubles in the past, then you may need to work on repairing your credit score. This can take a few years, but you can get around it if:

- You have a partner with a better credit score (let them buy the house)
- Both of you have bad scores; consider rental arbitrage or master leasing

My book, No Property, No Problem, details rental arbitrage; check it out if you find yourself in this situation. As for master leasing is very similar to house hacking, but you live in a *rental* instead of your property. You must ask for your landlord's permission before you master lease. Many will agree if you ask nicely and choose tenants they would have chosen anyway.

If you've been pre-approved for a loan, then it's go-time! Get that down payment ready because you're one step closer to purchasing a house.

Since you're living in the house, you get special down payment benefits. The bank you are speaking with will let you know the exact terms and specifics, but down payments can be as low as 3% for the general population. If you're active duty or a veteran, you might get a VA loan at a 0% rate.

Whatever you told the bank you'll pay as a down payment needs to be sitting in a bank account the day you close. Please do not put it in the stock market, bitcoin, or gold. These assets all work when investing long-term, but to buy a house within the next five years, you're better off placing it in a high-interest savings account. Banks won't accept bitcoin, gold, or stocks as a down payment either. And these investments can be a little hard to liquidate quickly - especially gold.

One quick note on visiting lenders: your credit score uses hard inquiries as one of their health metrics. Each time you ask a lender what interest rate they will give you, they perform another hard inquiry. All hard inquiries made within a 14-day period will only be counted as one, so get your ducks in a row and visit every bank, credit union, or other mortgage lender within 14 days.

Visit with multiple lenders; they will all pre-approve you for a slightly different rate. You want to go with the lender that balances the best interest rate and the highest loan amount.

You can go to www.automatedretirees.com/MortgageCalculator to figure out which loan is better. A 5% interest payment will have you paying significantly more than a 3% interest payment each month (and over the term of the loan). So, make sure you know exactly what your monthly payment is for each pre-approval letter before you decide which lender to use.

Now, let's consider what we need to know to create a great investment decision.

1. How much do we want to make each month? (This number should come from your monetary goal from your *why*.)
2. What do we need for a down payment?
3. What is our monthly payment going to be?
4. What is the maximum we can spend on a house?
5. What are the hidden expenses of owning a house?

Depending on your area, all of these might work together to help you reach your goal! However, there are a few more things you need to keep in the back of your head when investing in houses.

Some Business Bonuses

An operating fund, utilities, and taxes on rent are three major expenses that new investors often forget to think about before buying a house. If you don't understand these three things, then you will likely overspend.

The Importance of an Operating fund

This is an emergency fund for your house and differs from your tenant's deposit because that deposit can be used only when *they* damage your house. Like that time my brother-in-law was bringing his computer chair upstairs and slipped, punching a head-sized hole in the wall. The house was one day old, for crying out loud! Bam! Immediate use of his deposit.

The deposit will cover nothing your tenant did not directly cause - like structural damage. Last year, we had a lot of wind and rain; a few shingles on my roof lifted off. There's no way any of my tenants went on my roof and ripped off the shingles; it was 100% mother nature!

Your operating fund is for the times you can't blame your tenants. And it will happen, no matter how pristine you keep your house. So, don't neglect the operating fund!

Earlier, I said you should have $5,000 set aside for this purpose before purchasing the house. If saving this much is unfeasible for you, you can save it up after buying your house instead. It's a little riskier to do it that way, but it can be done. Meanwhile, I suggest you apply for a 0% APR credit card so you can put any emergency expenses on that card.

Once you have renters, save some of their rent each month to fill your fund. 10%-15% is a good goal. It's better to have some money on hand before you buy the house because. . .

The operating fund also covers *vacancies*.

If something drastic happens and you can't find someone to rent out one or more of your rooms, then your operating fund is there to cover the mortgage until you can. This situation usually happens just after you buy the home and haven't found tenants yet. Afterward, you can stipulate (in the lease) that tenants must give you 60 days advance notice before vacating.

Sixty days is a long time to find a new tenant, so you probably won't have an issue. But, on the off chance you do, you have your operating fund!

Who Pays for Utilities?

There are a few different ways you can split utilities with your tenants. You could "include it in their rent" and charge them a flat rental fee each month. That's the way I do it because it's easy, and I know how much my house uses each month in utilities. I also like that I can deduct from taxes what I spend on their share of utilities. I talk about this in-depth later in A

Mega Primer on Taxes, so don't worry if you don't know what that means right now.

The second option is to split the utilities evenly between all of you. I'm all about *easy*, and this way certainly isn't as easy as just including it in the rent. With this approach, you must look at your utility bill each month, divide it by two, and bill your tenants separately.

If you choose this approach, the money your tenants pay for utilities will be considered as part of rental income, and you must include it in your taxes. Still, you can also deduct what they spent on utilities. Confused? My A Mega Primer On Taxes includes information on this, so sit tight.

No matter which way you do it, you can deduct the amount you spent on their utilities from their taxes. And that's important because you'll technically "get that money back" at the end of the year. However, whatever utilities you use *personally* cannot be deducted.

A Mega Primer on Taxes

Property investors are levied with two taxes: property taxes and business/investment taxes. On its face, taxation seems complicated, but it's actually not too hard to understand. Remember, I'm not a lawyer or a CPA, and I don't live in your state (unless that state is Texas), so do your research. I also might not live in your country (unless that country is The USA), and tax codes are different for each country.

In the United States, the house you *live in* and a house you *invest in* have slightly different tax laws. Investment properties are considered a business in the US, so they get a lot of tax benefits.

The good news is, you are renting out a portion of your property, so you get some of these tax benefits! The bad news is that you only get to deduct the percentage of the home your renters use, not the entire property.

Let's say you have a two-bedroom/one-bath property with a living room and a kitchen. You could deduct one bedroom, half the bathroom, half the living room, and half the kitchen. In this scenario, whatever deductions you'd typically get for your property would be divided by two.

Alternatively, you can also do it by square feet. Normally, you get a floorplan when you purchase a house, providing the square feet in each room. You can include 100% of the square feet that your renters use 100% of the time, like their room, a game room, an office, etc.

You can portion out the other parts of the house at your own discretion. Try not to lie about it, but don't be too scared either.

It's not like the IRS will knock on your door and time how much you use the kitchen vs. your tenants. This is not an official term, but since I use this concept a lot, I will call this percentage your **P**rorated **D**eduction **A**mount (PDA).

Now, onward to deductions!

You can deduct your insurance payments, management fees, and any furniture you bought to furnish the common areas of your home at the PDA. If you buy furniture for your tenants, that is 100% deductible because they use it 100% of the time.

Any repairs you make to the house can also be deducted from a rental property. Remember that roof repair I talked about earlier? Deductible at the PDA! The repair for the sheetrock hole my brother-in-law made with his chair? That can also be deducted at the PDA because it was on the switchback stair landing – which is a *shared space*.

However, the damage he did to the towel rod can be 100% deducted (no PDA.) My brother-in-law broke *his own* towel rod, which is 100% deductible because I don't use their bathroom. Mercifully, I don't even clean it... the maids do that!

Speaking of that, a maid service is another deductible expense! So, if you hate cleaning, I have great news for you. To deduct the big significant full cleaning service, you can just hire maids to clean the areas your tenants occupy, making that cost 100% deductible. If you hire a maid to clean the whole house, you can deduct it only by the PDA.

Advertising, legal, and accounting fees can also be deducted at 100% because these are all activities you would only do for your business. So, if you wanted to hire an accountant to decipher complicated US tax law for you, then you can deduct that too! Because boy, it gets way more complicated - like the concept of standard depreciation.

The IRS considers a house a *depreciating asset* because, with time, certain wear-and-tear lowers the value. Obviously, you're going to take great care of your home because you understand that it is an *appreciating* asset that – as time passes – will be worth more than when you bought it.

$$Appreciation = sold\, price - buy\, price$$

The IRS understands that too, so there is a catch to this nice benefit that Uncle Sam has thrown us; it's called *the depreciation recapture tax*. More on that later!

The way depreciation works is . . .

Take the amount you pay for the house, subtract the value of the land, multiply that by your prorated deduction amount, and then multiply that number by real estate's standard depreciation rate of 3.636.

$$Depreciation = (Purchase\ Price - Value\ of\ Land) \times (prorated\ deduction\ amount) \times 3.636$$

You see that I've subtracted the value of the land from that equation. You can't depreciate the land; you can only depreciate the house. This is because the land will still be worth the same amount in the eyes of good old Uncle Sam when you're finished using it. So, you need to figure out what your land is worth and what your house is worth. You can use an accountant to do this, but you can also look at your local CAD (County Appraisal District) website. Usually, the government has already separated those two factors for your convenience. Just google CAD <my County>. Your county should have a website that asks for your name or address.

There is one hidden factor you should know about, just for posterity's sake. It's called the *depreciation period*. 27.5 years for a house built after 1986 and 31.5 years for a house built before. That means you must stop taking the depreciation tax break after your home's depreciation period.

One last thing, depreciation is only used for the PDA.

The other side of taxes is capitalization, aka the profit you make from your property. Like with a regular job, you will need to report your earnings from your rental to the IRS. Your earnings include rent, the money you used from the deposit to repair damages, and any other money your tenant used to pay for utilities or major repairs.

You might be confused because earlier, I said you could deduct the deposit from your tax burden – and you can. But you also have to claim it as rental income. Same with utilities. You can deduct the amount your tenant paid for utilities, but you also have to claim any payments your renters made towards utilities as rental income.

Even if your rental income is more than the total of your rental expenses, including depreciation, you may be able to carry forward some expenses. There is a nifty worksheet on the IRS's website you can fill out to determine what that number is if you're sadistic enough to do it yourself.

If you're in the US, I hope you picked up on this section's moral: Hire a CPA. The cost is tax-deductible and will save tens – if not hundreds – of hours of your time. There's also a lot less chance you will be audited if you use a pro. I just wanted you to be aware of the tax guidelines, *in general,* to include them in our calculations later.

There's also some bad news about renting out your house I feel like I need to mention. First, you can only deduct a portion of your interest expenses.

Usually, you can deduct money spent on interest from both personal and investment property payments. However, when you house hack, you have to split it up on your tax forms. Your PDA will go on a tax form called Schedule E (investment property tax form). The remaining percentage must go on a tax form called Schedule A (personal property tax form).

The problem lies in splitting this deduction up. Your itemized deductions need to be more than your standard deduction. Suppose the amount isn't significant enough to itemize on one or both of these. In that case, you must forego that benefit, taking just the standard deduction. So, you might lose out on some tax benefits.

The next downside concerns selling the house. When you sell a property, you have to pay taxes. One of them is on the depreciation you took over the years, called depreciation recapture. The second is the capital gains tax.

Let's talk about these.

Depreciation Recapture Tax

The depreciation recapture tax is based upon your personal tax rate. (Unlike the capital gains tax, which is based on the standard long-term capital gains tax rate for investing.)

These tax rates change all the time, so you must check for the updated rates if you're reading this book far in the future of when it was written. However, the general concept will probably remain the same, so here goes!

If you buy a house for $250,000 with the land being valued at $50,000, then the house is actually worth $200,000. For depreciation purposes, you'll multiply this number by your PDA. Let's just say that's 50% for now. You're left with $100,000. You multiply that by the standard deduction rate of 3.636%. You can deduct $3,636 per year.

If you sell it ten years after you bought it, you must pay taxes on the difference between what you said the house would be worth this year and the price you initially paid for it. If your house appreciated or stayed the same, Uncle Sam doesn't forget that you told him it was a *depreciating asset* – that means a difference in your sales tax.

Now that we've calculated our standard depreciation, we know how much depreciation we've had for the past ten years.

10 * $3,636 = $36,360

(years) * (depreciation amount) = (total depreciation)

The tax rate for depreciation depends upon owning entity's tax rate but is *(thankfully)* capped at 25%. For instance, if your personal tax rate is 12%, you only pay 12% on $36,360. However, if your tax rate is 32%, then you only pay 25%.

For this example, let's say you make $43,000 per year, which is at the higher end of the second tax bracket. Your personal tax rate is 12%, and your long-term capital gains tax rate is 15%. So, you pay $4,363 in depreciation recapture taxes (15%) when you sell.

Now, on to the second part of *taxes you pay when you sell.*

Capital Gains

Anyone who invests in any asset pays taxes on capital gains. That includes people who invest in the stock market, gold, or other commodities. To briefly explain capital gains, there are two tax rates, short-term and long-term.

Since you're very unlikely to experience a short-term capital gain on a house (you'd have to sell your home within one year of purchasing it to qualify for the expensive short-term capital gains taxes), I will only talk about the long-term capital gains tax.

The brackets for the long-term capital gains tax also change, so I'm not even going to put the percentage you're likely to pay; I'll just say it is usually lower than your personal tax rate.

In most cases, Uncle Sam rewards long-term investors by giving them an advantageous tax rate.

Let's say you will sell your house for $500,000 now. 50% ROI over ten years is pretty respectable! Nice job . . .

. . . except now you need to pay taxes on your gains.

Capital gains tax differs from depreciation because you pay it on both the house *and* the land. You pay it on *any house* you sell, whether it's an investment or owner-occupied. So, for simplicity, we'll calculate capital gains on your entire home, not just the PDA.

Capital gains are equal to the difference between what you paid for and what you sold it for:

$500,000 - $250,000 = $250,000

Hey, I didn't make the tax rules! Don't blame me!

So, you will multiply your appreciation by your long-term capital gains tax rate, which we established was 15% in this example.

$250,000 * .15 = $37,500.

But wait, there's more! And this time, it's *good* news.

If you lived in the house for at least two of the last five years, you could file a form called section 121 that excludes you from paying capital gains on profits of up to $250,000. You can only apply that to the portions of the house you owner-occupied. So, essentially, you'll multiply $37,500 by your PDA. That gives us $18,750 less in capital gains tax.

Since you house hacked, you have $4,363 in depreciation + $18,750 from capital gains. You'll have to pay $23,113 in taxes when you sell.

But wait! There's more good news.

There is also another tax advantage called the 1031 exchange. This allows you to defer the taxes you'll pay on an investment property's capital gains tax as long as you purchase another investment property. Therefore. as long as you buy another investment property (within a specific timeframe; call your tax advisor), you don't have to pay that extra $18,750.

This leaves you with a tax bill of $4,363. If you had the house for ten years, you probably made more than that in your rental income, so I wouldn't be too worried about it. *(I'd rather just take out a HELOC loan and use that to buy whatever I wanted to buy!)*

So, back to the topic at hand. What does all this tax stuff mean for our monthly expenses? And why have I spent so long talking about it if I just want you to speak to a CPA?

How to Live for Free

Well, the answer to the second question is #KnowledgeIsPower.

As for the first, tax deductions are pretty simple on their face. *(Pshh . . . where have I said that before?)* Still, they are necessary to establish your true profit when considering a house for hacking.

This is best learned in table format; for my fellow visual learners, I'll put the rest of my explanation in table form.

Let's say you managed to get your hands on a duplex, so your PDA is 50%. You charge your renter $1,300 for their unit. They pay their own utilities. That comes out to $15,600 in rent each year. You bought the duplex for $250,000 at a 3.5% interest rate for 30 years.

	Annual Total	Deductible by Schedule E (Investment deductions)	Deductible by Schedule A (Personal deductions)	Nondeductible
Property taxes	$7,500	$3,750		$3,750
Mortgage interest **	$8,600	$4,300	$4,300	
Insurance	$1,000	$500		500
Utilities paid	$3,000	$1,500		$1,500

Maintenance and repairs	$1,000	$750***		$250
Other Common Expenses (Maids, lawn service, etc.)	$1,500	$750		$750
Depreciation	$9,900	$9,900		
Total	$32,500	$21,450	$4,300	$6750

** Mortgage interest is amortized. That means you pay less interest each year.

*** This number assumes all the damage in their sections and PDA damage in the common areas.

So, let's put all of this together.

Gross rents = $15,600

Total rental expenses, before depreciation = $21,450

Rental Expenses + Personal Deductions = $25,750

Net income, before depreciation (cash flow) = -$4,300

Depreciation = $9,900

Net loss (no taxable rental income) = $14,200

That net loss number looks kind of scary, but you actually want that number to be above zero because when it's *below* zero, you pay taxes on your rental income. If the house were not depreciating at all, you'd have to pay taxes on the $4,050 gain from rent. But, since you're *losing* in the eyes of the law, WHAM! No taxes!

Tax-free rent, baby!

Later on, when we create our calculator, we'll try to create it to run our business at a loss every year. Sometimes, you can carry this loss forward, but that's outside of this book's scope and not my expertise.

That's pretty much all I have for you on taxes! Now we can finally move onto something more fun.

TL;DR

That's a lot to remember as you search for a house or structure your own business. At the beginning of this book, the free gifts I included have a rental calculator that will help you determine profit with any house. A tax deduction section enables you to determine whether you'll be operating at a net loss (on paper), allowing you to forego any taxes on incoming rent.

If you're a little confused about taxes, my advice is to hire a CPA to explain everything to you. They're helpful, and the cost can be deducted from your expenses! They'll also be able to give you a list of the other tax deductions you can take; that list is vast.

Part 2

Buying Your House Hacking Heaven and Finding Angels for Tenants

CHAPTER 3

Purchasing a New House

If you don't own a home, buy one. If you own a home, buy another one. If you own two homes, buy a third. And lend your relatives the money to buy a home.

~ John Paulson

What You Can Expect From This Chapter

- *Which areas are better for house hacking*
- *Why your realtor is an essential member of your team and how to find the best one*
- *A guide to all the fees associated with buying a house (even the ones they don't tell you about)*

We Bought a House!

I've rented and house hacked a lot of different properties over the years, most notably in my final college semester. Like many responsible young adults, I waited until the *very last second* to break my lease from the semester before. I had a good reason: my previous apartment smelled, was in a bad neighborhood, and had hot water only in one of the showers. It was pretty much the definition of a cheap place to live, and I had shared it with another student who had moved on to greener pastures.

Instead of looking for a new roommate, I reasoned that I'd find another place to live. I'd had a lot of housemate experience over the past four years and thought that I'd be able to handle anything fate threw at me.

I also thought I'd be able to find a new place to stay with no issues. Of course, I didn't want to pay a deposit before I knew that I could wiggle out of my current lease, so I didn't even try to find a new place to live until that was settled.

Boy, was it a mistake to make those two assumptions!

The next day-and-a-half consisted of me calling every apartment I could find on Google in that tiny college town. Almost nothing had availability . . . but they all had waiting lists!

Now, as a property owner myself, I can't blame them. After all, it was the end of June.

Two waiting lists later, my heart started sinking. Five waiting lists later, and I wondered if I would even get to attend college that semester. Ten waiting lists later – and I was becoming ok with the idea of sleeping under a bridge or making my home in the 24/7 library. It was my last semester, and I was determined to do whatever it took to graduate!

Thankfully, I had spent the last four years making friends. So, I started calling them. Almost none had space. We were all too poor for the luxury of more space than we needed! However, one of them had just moved in with her boyfriend! They had found a one-bedroom apartment. Bingo!

We arranged for my bedroom to be a portion of their living room. I looked at privacy curtains, white noise machines, and bedrolls. It wasn't ideal, but it was better than a bridge!

Thankfully, enough people dropped out of one of the apartment complexes; I finally got my own room.

My friend proved that you can house hack anything if you're creative enough! That said, it *does* depend on your personal privacy level, goals, and physical house. Thankfully, my friend had just gotten out of the military, so she was used to sharing small spaces with a lot of people. It can be done if you're willing to do it. Even if your house has only a few rooms, you can find other places to rent out.

Of course, if you're starting from scratch and looking for a new house, then you have your pick of whatever is in your budget.

How To Find A Desirable Area

Since you're house hacking, you're limited to a city you can live in. I find that the best places to house hack are the suburbs, not city centers or rural areas. You must also pay attention to the crime level in your chosen area; you will not attract quality renters if you live in an unsafe neighborhood.

By far, the best way to know if crime is happening in an area near you is to *live near it.* Everyone has a very sharp sense of safe and unsafe; remember that *one street* can separate good and bad areas.

There's always going to be some crime; no matter what, there will be some petty theft, vandalism, and even a few assaults. As long as there is no murder and there is a minimum of house break-ins, the area should be fine.

If you need to move into a new city, then the second-best way to check for crime is to use spotcrime.com. This gives an excellent overview of the crime in the past few months. Once I've settled on an area, I use Trulia's crime maps to determine if the house I'm looking at is in a high-crime area. I like Trulia.com better because it uses a heatmap, but Trulia only shows you crime around a specific house. *(It works better when you already have a place in mind rather than when you're canvassing.)*

Nearby Jobs

You also need to consider the types of available jobs nearby. You can house hack in almost any area, but the quality of employment in the area significantly affects renter quality.

For instance, if you live near a hospital or tech hub, you'll probably get nurses and electrical or computer engineers. These individuals usually have a higher credit score, are quiet, and are relatively clean. They have also proven that they can pay their debt on time because they paid for college.

We will discuss things like this at length in the next chapter, but the closer your house is to tech companies, hospitals, and business centers, the more likely you will find tech workers, hospital staff, and businesspeople to rent your house. You can rent to whoever you'd like, but professionals will typically have less drama and enough money to cover rent every month.

You might believe that these types of people make too much money to want to rent a room. While it's true that they make enough money to get by, everyone starts at a different place, and these individuals are usually saddled with college debt they need to pay off. Some might even be saving for a down payment of their own. So, it just makes sense they would look for safe, clean, cheap housing until they've hit their goal.

Market Value of Rent

The next thing to closely consider is the rent in the area. I like to use Facebook Marketplace because it's extremely popular, and I can see how long other postings have been left up. If I monitor it for a few days, it's easy to determine what an area's room generally goes for – or if house hacking is even *feasible*.

Facebook Marketplace has a section explicitly targeting rooms for rent. You need to do only a little competitor research. Search for a zip code in your area and then peruse the price of rooms in that zip code, noting:

- **The bathroom situation.** Is it a shared bathroom or a private bathroom?
- **The room situation.** Make sure you're only looking at rent by the room, not the entire house (unless you're renting an entire unit of a multiplex. Then, look at that.)
- **The utilities.** Are they included in the price of rent? Or are they paid separately?

- **Amenities.** Those extra little goodies that your renters get when they rent a room at your house can make a difference. These can include a pool, hot tub, walking trails, dog park, bus routes, major highways, and a wardrobe that opens to Narnia. Anything that you like about your neighborhood or home that other homes or communities in your area don't have is an *amenity*.

- **Size of room.** Bigger rooms will go for slightly more. The master bedroom in my house is twice the size of the other bedrooms. That doesn't mean I get to charge twice the rent, but it does mean I can charge a few hundred dollars more.

- **Pictures.** Are there good pictures of the space on MarketPlace? Good pictures usually result in better renters. Presentation is everything!

I've found that the number of rooms in a house rarely affects a room's price too much. So, a five-bedroom house versus a three-bedroom house would rent their rooms for about the same price –as long as the bathrooms, amenities, and utilities are accounted for.

Also, check out the quality of the rental itself. Is it in a better area than yours? Is it decorated better? Does the house just look more custom or luxurious?

The number of days the listing has been posted is another good indication of the price you can charge. These listings are usually still there because people have not rented them yet. So, to get the best picture in terms of price in your area, check back every day for a few days.

You'll notice that some rooms rent and others don't. If you keep an eye on it for a while, you might notice that rooms above a certain price don't rent out. Or maybe ugly listings aren't renting. Whatever the case, as long as you keep your eye on it, you'll be able to determine the best price for your space.

I've created a free excel sheet to help you track the rooms in an area (*check for the link at the front of this book.*) This handy tool enables you to decide how much to charge per room.

Once you know how much you can charge per room, you'll learn how much you will make each month. Plug this number into the free calculator *(also included with this book)* along with the information from your lender, and you'll be ready to determine your perfect house for hacking.

Now that you know what you want, you can talk to a realtor!

The Importance of a Great Realtor (And Where to Find One)

Finding a good realtor is an art. There are good and bad realtors, and like any profession, realtors need to have a variety of skills. You're looking for that professional that gives you advice when you need it, negotiates a great deal, and knows how to close them! Most of these skills come with experience.

First, ask your friends and families for references. Word of mouth from people you trust is the best way to find great professionals in the service industry.

The realtor I use has a zero online presence, but he's been helping his clients buy and sell houses for almost 30 years! He's such a great realtor that he doesn't need to create a website to capture leads - he gets them all via word of mouth.

Just like that super little hole-in-the-wall Mexican restaurant, you'll find the best realtors may not have an online presence. Their superb work speaks for itself, and their careers take off because they're honest and good at their job.

Word of mouth is better. Multiple people telling you a realtor is amazing: the best.

But what if you don't know of any realtors in the area? What do you do then?

Our next best tool is the internet. But we aren't just going to look at a Realtor's star ratings to determine if they're worth their salt or not. We're going to dig a little bit deeper.

One of the gifts God has given investors is Zillow. The great creators of Zillow have thought of almost everything, and the app only gets better and more accurate each year. Now, Zillow has a section specifically designed for you to pick through all the realtors in your area.

If you were an investor looking to rent out a house you didn't live in, you'd have broader options in terms of location. Since you're bound by your job, family, or whatever else, you need to pick a nearby property.

Realtors are only licensed to work in specific zip codes, but luckily, those are usually conjoined – all in the same area. So, if you straddle the line between two zip codes, it's likely your realtor can still help you.

It's still a good idea to know which neighborhoods you would like to invest in. This will narrow down your realtor's search significantly and will save you both a bunch of time. No matter what realtor you pick, if you're in the US, they'll probably set you up on an MLS drip. MLS stands for **M**ultiple **L**isting **S**ervice - the official listing service for houses being sold by realtors.

As an individual, you don't have access to this unless you go through a realtor.

The MLS is a very cool and helpful tool. Realtors can input your desired metrics down to the very street. If the only thing you're willing to consider purchasing is a 3/2 (3-bedroom/ 2-bath condo on Cherry Street, they can set up that specific drip for you! While that almost guarantees nothing that matches your criteria, that's not your realtor's fault. They're just setting up the drip.

Once you find a house you'd like to buy, the real skill of the realtor comes into play. They will take you into the neighborhood and show you around. (The realtor I use, David, happened to be an old family friend *and* an amazing realtor.)

When my husband and I finally had enough money for a down payment, David took us shopping. I had spent the last three months looking at slightly-loved homes, finding five I thought would be nice to live in with Eddy, his brother Al, and Al's long-time girlfriend, Kris.

Eddy and I looked at all five of these houses with David that day. It was pretty fun at first, but as we toured, I began seeing a pattern; all the homes in my price range were . . . well, they weren't *loved;* they were *used*.

My heart dropped a little with each house. The rental we were living in at the time was in a cute neighborhood. It was a 4/3.5 and was perfect for our current situation. At least, it was miles ahead of any of the houses I tried to buy that day!

By day's end, David said that *he* had picked a few houses for us to tour. He thought they were in our price range, new, and would match our particular situation. After all, he and I had talked at length about what I was looking for.

Low and behold, the third house we visited that day was the one Eddy and I bought. It was only $20,000 more than the used homes we had looked at, but it was new, had twice the space, and was in a nice area.

I'm not sure how he found this house or how we got so lucky, but thank goodness we had a great realtor! He also talked the sales realtor into giving us a free washer and dryer and paying all the closing fees. In the end, we got a sweet, sweet deal.

How can you find your own David?

Zillow makes it easy for us to find real estate agents and look at reviews; just go to https://www.zillow.com/agent-finder and type in your desired zip code.

Zillow focuses on residential real estate, so there are only two realtors you have to worry about: buyers and sellers. By the way, since you are buying a house, you need to find a *buyer's agent* (be sure to indicate that in the dropdown box *Service Needed*.)

Hundreds of brokerages and agents will pop up, c conveniently sorted by star ranking! Spend 10 to 20 minutes going through some of the five-star ratings of a few agents you like. Once you've narrowed your list down, set up phone calls with three.

When you call these agents, you want to size them up. In my opinion, the most critical question to answer is: do you trust them? You will be spending a good chunk of time (and a lot of money!) with whichever agent you choose, so you need to make sure they pass your internal sniff test. Do they seem trustworthy? Will they do a good job? Do they know a lot about the area?

When you meet your first real estate agent, you probably won't know what to say. Maybe you'll even feel a little bit star-struck! Nah . . . probably not, unless you meet one of the realtors from *Selling Sunset*, the Netflix show where half of the realtors are TV stars, and they all sell mansions worth six million dollars or more!

At any rate, here is a general flow for your interview.

First, introduce yourself! Realtors pride themselves on being personable, so expect them to immediately figure out what your favorite hobby is and know just as much about it as you do! After the first five minutes of an interview, any realtor worth their salt will feel like an old friend – *screen for this positive quality.*

Once you've gotten to know each other, tell them a little bit about what you're trying to do: buy your first house, but one big enough to rent out a few rooms to your friends.

Below is an extensive list of questions; ask them all!

Q: How well do you know this area?

The answer must be: VERY well. The better they know the area, the more they can help you. For instance, when I worked with David, he helped me avoid builders not up to par with the builder I wound up buying from. He also had insider knowledge of the real estate being sold. A realtor who isn't as familiar with the area must rely solely on the MLS. The MLS is fine, but inside knowledge is much better! Your realtor might even know about houses before they come on the market.

Q: How many houses did you help people buy last year? And how many were in this area?

This is a great follow-up question to the one you just asked. Top agents can do 40-50 transactions in a year, while average agents will do around 20. You want to make sure you're working with a top agent who has done at least ten transactions in the last 12 months *in the area you're looking in*. This almost guarantees they know the area well because they successfully helped ten people find a house in your target area.

Q: How long have you been a realtor?

You want this answer to be *over* five years. New realtors have their place, but you are trying to buy your first home to find the *right* home for your *unique* situation. A realtor with more experience will probably have seen this exact situation before and will have more insight into the things you will need for a house hack. They might even be able to give you advice!

Q: Is this your full-time job?

Some realtors are in the middle of exiting one career and entering another one. Unfortunately, if that's the case for your realtor, you will need to pass. If they have another job, they aren't going to be as focused on real estate. So, you must focus on full-time realtors. They'll have more time to spend zeroing in on *you* and knowing more about the area and real estate in general. They just have more space in their brain for real estate!

Q: On average, how many houses do you show each of your clients before they buy?

The lower the number, the better. Especially if you have a full-time job and other responsibilities. The fewer houses a realtor shows you, the better they realize and match their clients' wants and needs.

When I went wedding dress shopping, I was paired with a lady named Marissa. She was part-owner of the store and had helped thousands of brides-to-be find their wedding dresses. In my mind, wedding dress shopping would be a huge ordeal that would take me months. After all, I was spending thousands on a *dress*! That's a *huge* decision. Fortunately for me, I was paired with Marissa, who asked me a few questions, showed me a few pictures of dresses, then went to pick a few out for me.

Three tries; that's all it took she found the one. I had a dress in one day instead of months. And that's exactly what you want to look for in a realtor. You want to find your real estate Marissa because she will help you find your perfect investment as quickly as possible!

Q: How do you determine which homes might be a match for me?

An intake form or interview is fine, but in my experience, the best realtors show you some in-stock real estate, inviting you to their office to see a few houses on the market while they get to know you and your goals. You won't physically go see each house during that meeting; you'll just see pictures and features. This is a lot better than an intake form because they will pick up minute details they may not have known otherwise, making it easier for them to formulate your perfect house in their minds.

The clearer their vision of your perfect house, the less time everyone wastes. Driving around and looking at homes is a very time-consuming task. It can take 20 minutes to an hour just to drive to a property in your area. If they take you to ten duds, that's ten hours – wasted!

Q: How do you provide us with information on these homes?

In general, they should be sending you full listings from the MLS –*that may vary for countries outside the US*. At a bare minimum, they should send you the address, the number of rooms and bathrooms, the square footage, and a few pictures.

An important related question: how often do they give you information? Will they call every time there's a new deal, or wait until the end of the month and then text you with them?

If you are in a very hot market, then you may want him to call you with new deals *as* they come available. Look, if houses are selling on the same day they're listed, then speed is everything. But, if it's a slow market, an email each morning with all the new listings fitting your criteria should work just fine.

Q: Do you attend inspections?

Top buyer's agents attend the inspections. Think about it: they go through hundreds, if not thousands, of homes in their career. They know the builders, the quality to expect, and have a keen eye for things that might be wrong.

Let's say you buy a car on Craigslist. If you know nothing about cars, wouldn't you feel a whole lot better if your buddy (who tunes them for fun) comes along? Even though he's not a mechanic (just like a realtor isn't a builder), he spends a lot of his time looking at – and maybe working on – cars. He watches tons of videos; he knows how they work, what's expected, and what isn't. Like your realtor with houses!

Q: How do you negotiate our requests after inspections?

Unless already stated on the sales listing, items your inspector finds in your prospective purchase can be used to negotiate the price down! Either the sellers will need to fix it, or they will need to give you enough of a discount to fix it.

It's just like buying a car. If you go on Craigslist and find your dream car, you'd expect it to be as advertised. If you discover it's missing the rearview mirror, you're going to haggle the price down.

Q: How do you get paid, and do I have to sign anything to work with you?

In the United States, realtors get paid a commission. In Texas, each agent gets 3% of the purchase price. It may vary by state, so it's always good to ask.

Also, you rarely have to sign a contract stating that you'll work with them exclusively. If it's common in your area, then you may. If it's not, don't make an exception just to work with *whoever this random guy is*.

A simple 15-minute phone conversation should be enough to answer all of these questions, along with any follow-ups you might have. Speak to at least three realtors before deciding on your House Hacking Dream Team's new member.

That's another tip. You need to think of your realtor as a *member of your team*. Just like your lender. If all goes well, you'll be using their services again in a few years to buy another house. Finding the right realtor now makes it that much easier later on; when you're ready to buy another house, just pick up the phone!

The Hidden Fees No One Tells You About

After your realtor helps you find the perfect house, it's time to sign on the dotted line for the agreed price, right? When Eddy and I bought our first house, we didn't know about the extra fees associated with the purchase *aside from the down payment*, things like earnest money and closing fees.

Nevertheless, we ventured out into the fantastical world of real estate anyway. My father has always kept up with real estate because he's always loved the idea of investing . . . he just never pulled the trigger! In 2018, he told us that the real estate market was getting ready to explode and that we needed to buy a house *now*. Otherwise, we might get stuck waiting another few years while the market calmed down.

So, we worked on saving enough money to buy one. By the end of 2018, we had a paltry $10,000 saved up. That's right, ten grand for an entire house. We contacted David and got busy searching!

You already know how David helped us find our perfect house, but you don't know about the fiasco afterward! We started looking at houses on January 28th. By January 29th, we'd already found one and put down a $1,000 earnest fee.

The earnest fee is a non-refundable fee you, the buyer, pay the seller when you officially sign the paperwork indicating you intend to buy their house. This money represents your stake in the contract. If you back out, you lose your earnest fee. Everyone shakes on it, and both sides come away happy. The seller knows they are due some consolation if the buyer walks away; the buyer knows that the seller is legally barred from selling their house to anyone else.

If you are purchasing your first house (congrats!), then you'll get special deals like a 3% down FHA loan for a 6% interest rate. (*This is a special deal because of the low down payment, not because of the interest rate. That interest rate is horrendous.*)

You should already know about your rates because you spoke with your lender and got preapproved earlier – before you looked at and fell in love with your new house. They usually give you a variety of loans to choose from.

Generally, you want to strike a balance between a low interest rate and an affordable monthly payment. If you can stomach it, the lower interest rate will give you the most house for your cash in the long run, but if you aren't buying a mega 7-room mansion, the 30-year conventional loan or the FHA loan are probably the two that will work best with your budget.

Hopefully, you're close to saving the amount you needed to save for your down payment. If you just need a little extra oomph, I have a neat trick for you.

If you've read my book *Beach House Business Model*, you can probably guess what I'm about to say next; I am in love with 0% interest rate credit cards. In a nutshell, these cards act like regular credit cards but have an 8-to-18-month promotional period where you pay no interest. It is in your best interest to pay this card off *before* that promotional term comes to an end, or you will have to pay the standard, nasty high-interest rates on your balance.

Now, I'm not suggesting you try to use these cards to pay for your down payment; that is not allowed. However, you can use these cards for your living expenses for the time being and use all of that money for your down payment plus closing costs.

Speaking of closing costs, yours may differ from mine, but in general, they include:

- Application fee
- Appraisal fee

- Credit check fee
- Escrow (taxes and insurance for a few months, if required)
- Origination and/or underwriting fees
- Title insurance
- Title search fee
- Transfer tax (if applicable)

The total costs range from 2% to 5% of the *loan principal*, aka your *purchase price*. So, when you save a down payment, also factor in the closing costs.

Usually, your closing costs can and will be rolled into the loan, leaving you with just the bill for the down payment. However, it is good to know that they exist.

TL;DR

Figuring out what kind of house you will buy is pretty simple. Since you know your goals and the type of real estate out there, you have only to do a cost analysis. Once you've completed that research (and know the kind of house and what you can afford), start saving for – or buying – it! Step 1: Find your dream realtor. Step 2: Find your dream house by touring some properties. Step 3: Having found it, put down your earnest fee and sign the contract showing your intention to buy.

That's when your loan company comes in. Most reputable real estate transactions require pre-approval before you pay earnest fees and sign the offer-to-buy contract. If you aren't pre-approved and you can't find a lending company to lend you money in time, then you'll likely lose your earnest fee – and worse, the house.

Sometimes, you will get discounts for using the seller's loan company - especially if it's a builder. They have a loan company they like to work with, giving you discounts for using them. However, it's usually best to be pre-approved by your own company; at the very least, you have a backup.

Processing the loan usually takes a few months, so the closing is not immediate. While you're waiting, there's an inspection and usually, some negotiation based on that inspection's results. It's best if you and your realtor go to the inspection. You can help the inspector notice issues – and learn a little bit about houses while you're there.

Once the inspection is complete, all negotiations are made, and the loan has been processed, you get to close! Closing entails sitting down at a title company or attorney's office, signing an entire ream of paperwork, and handing over a wad of cash (money order or wire transfer) for the down payment and closing costs. You can't pay them with a credit card.

Then, you own a house, and the real fun begins!

** A quick note. The sellers in Texas have to pay way more closing costs. Generally, they pay 6% in closing costs and the 6% realtor commission fee (3% for the buyer's agent and 3% for the seller's agent). Yet another reason as to why I get HELOCs on my properties instead of selling them. More on that in another book!

CHAPTER 4

The Zero Stress Tenant Vetting System

Real estate is the purest form of entrepreneurship.

~Brian Buffini

What You Can Expect From This Chapter

- *What makes a perfect tenant (and where you find them)*
- *Creating a tantalizing listing causing all nearby renters to want your space*

Does the perfect tenant even exist?

I woke up at about 3 pm one bleak Sunday afternoon. I was in college, so the first thing that ran through my head was, *why am I awake so early?* I liked to follow the sleep schedule advice of the great productivity hacker, *Procrastium.* He encouraged you to procrastinate, party, and worry about sleep when you were dead. So, I usually wasted Sundays sleeping in.

Don't clutch your pearls at me; I was an A+ student in an engineering field! We like parties too, we just don't have time for them, good grades, *and* sleep. At least, not all on the same day!

After a bit of soul searching, I rolled out of bed, looking for some clean clothes – without luck. . *Time to do the laundry.*

Lucky for me, we had a washer and dryer in our apartment. I say *our* because I shared this one with three other girls. One girl, I heard, existed because she loved to make messes, and another one I saw way too much; she just sat in the living room all the time and bugged anyone with the audacity to come out.

I packed my laundry up into the hamper and made my way down the stairs. I lived on the top floor of a 4-bedroom townhouse. The washing machine - and everything else, for that matter - might as well have been on Mars for how much interest I had in going up and down two flights of narrow switchback stairs. But when duty calls, you've gotta' answer.

When I got down to the washing machine, roommate C – who had taken over the main room – was blasting some kind of documentary on dogs. Usually, I like dogs, but this documentary sure had a ton of howling. I glanced at the kitchen and noticed that it was in its usual state: food warzone. I had never seen the kitchen clean, often opting to cook all my food at a friend's house every Sunday. Once, I watched a pot full of beans rot on the stove over the course of a few days. At least the stove was *off*.

But no, I thought, *I can't get distracted by the kitchen now. I don't want roommate C to catch me down here.* I turned my attention to the washing machine. *Good, there's nothing in it. That means I can wash my clothes!*

I open it up.

It is full of something I can only describe as a white foam. *What?*

"Hey, Roomie! Oh, yeah, the washing machine. Yeah, Roommate A ran out of laundry detergent, so I told her to give dishwasher soap a try. It didn't really work out . . ."

That year was full of life lessons that go way deeper than picking out the perfect tenant for house hacking.

So, does the perfect tenant exist? I've selected over 15 people to be my roommate over the years. Some were angels, and others were definitely something else. I learned a lot about who I like living with, how much dirt I can tolerate, and how to identify people that will always have an excuse as to why they simply can't pay me.

Your perfect tenant does exist. He or she is out there, and they may even be someone else's nightmare tenant! You need to find people who jibe with *you*.

Your Perfect Tenant

Before you can select a tenant, you need to have a heart-to-heart with yourself. What can you put up with? What do you care about? What will you absolutely *not* tolerate?

Q1: How clean are you?

On a scale of 1 to 10, how clean are you?

Do you wash your dishes, clean your counter and sweep your floor every night after dinner? Do you need all the pillows on every couch to remain where they are at all costs? Do you have a nervous breakdown when you see a dirty dish in the sink for more than an hour? If you answered yes, you're a 10.

Do you never wash your baseboards? If you eat something in your bedroom, do you place that dirty plate on top of a stack of other dishes (that are all in different states of molding)? If you run out of clean clothes, do you just reuse the one that smells the best? If yes, you're a 1.

Typically, people are somewhere in the middle of these two extremes, but your roommates can and will be closer to one than the other. Some people are fine with their kitchens being in a perpetual state of war. Others would rather live clean or die trying. You need to make sure you find roommates that have the same level of dedication as you.

For instance, I have a very lovely, discount boudoir in my entryway. We use it to hold all our shoes because our floors are made of cheap wood and get dirty if you even think about walking on them.

I like *all* shoes to be *in* this cabinet and for the carefully decorated cabinet to be *just so*. I want traveling salespeople and neighbors to look into my house's entryway and believe that I have my act together.

My roommates do not care to keep up this type of appearance, often using my beautifully decorated shoe rack as a place to put any random things they walk in with. Guitar cases, computers, headphones, and drinks all find their way onto my decorations. Sometimes, they even get to live there for a little while.

I realize I may sound a bit OCD here, but I'm simply trying to illustrate a point! This is something that I *like* to remain clean – something my roommates don't and won't understand, regardless of the dozens of times I've explained it.

Things like this will happen, and while you may not be able to hold them accountable for small things like *don't put your dirty stuff on my entryway furniture, you can* hold them to bigger things like *do your dishes when you use them!* Or *don't leave dirty plates in your room so long that they mold!*

Bottom line: be sure you screen for cleanliness levels when you interview your roommates; living with Pig-Pen is the #1 problem for house hackers.

A 6 and 9 can live together peacefully, so don't go overboard when you screen for cleanliness, or you'll never actually *pick a tenant*. If this is something you're worried about, a maid goes a long way towards easing the tension. Just make sure they're willing to put up with a maid coming once a month.

There is one issue I have yet to solve: them putting their random stuff everywhere. But that problem is what I like to call a *nice-to-have* problem; to me, it's such a minor issue that I'll gladly bear with it to keep my roommates around.

Q2: What do you consider fair use of the house?

On a scale from 1 to 10, how much do you want to see your roommate and their friends?

Do you cringe if your roommate is always in the living room? Does your sleep schedule become significantly affected if your roommate is loud at random hours of the day and night? Do you want exclusive use of the kitchen when *you* want to use it? You would be a 1.

Do you encourage your roommate to put their Xbox in the living room and – for all practical purposes – live *there* instead of their room? Do you want them to throw parties so you can meet all their friends (and you don't even care when! You're always down to par-tay!) Do you want to cook with your roommates so you bond? You're a 10.

If you've never lived with anyone else, *fair use of the house* is another concept you may not have thought about. Everyone has a different idea of what constitutes rudeness. For instance, Roommate C (I mentioned her earlier) was always in the main room doing whatever she wanted to do. She liked it! She actively *wanted* to see all of her roommates.

I didn't; I'd preferred to pretend like those ladies didn't exist.

I'm closer to a 1 on the fair use question; the less I see my roommates, the better. Because of this, I've set my house up, so we need not see each other if we don't want to. The only true shared space is the kitchen, but we have offset our dinner times to avoid that issue most of the time. Otherwise, they have their separate room, office, and living room.

Know how much you want to see of your roommates, making it clear from the beginning. We'll talk more about these rules in the next chapter.

Q3: How Do Guests Work?

The people you rent your house to are people too – and they'll likely want to have guests over. You'll need to be ok with that in some capacity because no one will rent from you if you aren't.

But that doesn't mean you can't have rules! Can the guest stay in your guest bedroom? Can the guests and your roommate use the common areas? Does your roommate need to clear with you before they have guests over?

These are questions to ask yourself before making a tenant deal. You aren't their mom, so you can't stop them from having guests, but determine your comfort level with guests and which parts of the house they can use.

This is also a good time to talk about significant others.

Most of the time, people renting rooms are single. Are you ok with their Tinder dates coming over? And what if their relationship status changes from *single* to *in a relationship*? That can make their rental status shift to *it's complicated.*

A few nights here or there with their significant other is no big deal (*that's barely enough time for me to start poking fun at them!*) However, if that same person stays over for over two weeks, you're facing a hard decision.

Are you renting by the room – or by *the person*?

Twice the people in one room amounts to twice the wear for that area: something worth considering. US tenant protection laws prevent you from kicking someone out without significant legal work – even if they aren't listed on the lease.

For most states, if your tenant's guest stays for 30 days, they're legally your tenant. If they're trying to punish your tenant by not leaving, then you will need to go through eviction to evict them legally; otherwise, they can sue you.

No matter your decision regarding surprise guests staying beyond a few weeks, it's wise to add them to the lease. That way, they're legally on the hook for any damages they've made, and it makes it easier to evict them later.

Q4: Splitting up purchases and chores

I once had a helpless roommate who – outside of a cup of ramen noodles – couldn't cook food for himself. We agreed that I would cook everything, but we'd split the food bill. This worked out fine for us, but eventually, we went our separate ways because of Question #1.

You don't want to know what I found in his room after he left .

You've got to decide whether to split up purchases and chores beforehand, making sure your tenants can live up to the agreement. Will you all put a little money into a pool each month for shared items in the household like trash bags, detergent, etc.? *(A complete "Shared Household List" is one of the free gifts listed at the beginning of this book!)* Or are you going to raise the rent a smidge more so you can buy them? Or maybe it's everyone for themselves! Decide these things, and make sure that these are spelled out in the tenancy agreement before signing up roommates.

In my earlier story about living with those three girls (the washing machine debacle) . . . I didn't get to pick those roommates, as it was the semester in which I was nearly homeless. Those pots that they used to destroy the kitchen? *Mine*, and the only thing I shared with them because it was too late *not to*! If only I'd known . . .

Everything else was up in my room. We didn't even share the trash can.

After deciding which items and chores are shared, ensure – in writing –that your roommates are up for that. If you don't plan on taking out the trash every week, mowing the lawn twice a month, and shoveling snow on your own, you must find roommates who agree to help with those –or roll the higher fees for having these chores done by professionals into their rent.

Now that you've interviewed yourself, you know a bit more about who you're looking for; let's go find some roomies!

New Tenants and Where to Find Them

Gone are the days where landlords and tenants could meet each other through a newspaper classified section. Nowadays, most interaction between landlords and tenants is done digitally via apps or the internet.

Renters are looking for more than just a lousy listing, describing the number of bedrooms and bathrooms. Apps let the tenants see what they're missing out on when they pick one listing over another; there are even walkthroughs of the house and surrounding area.

Your potential tenants want to see the property's videos, photos, and a map showcasing how close they could live to local attractions and cool amenities. You can't just have a nice listing; you also need to promote it on high-traffic platforms. Here are my top seven platforms for finding long-term and medium-term tenants.

Facebook

For long-term, rent-by-the-room tenants, Facebook is my go-to! I find the quality of people on Facebook to be much higher than most other apps – except for Airbnb. Plus, it's free!

When people respond to your ad on Facebook, they will be answering as themselves, and they have a profile you can usually find to check them out, making this a quality approach.

Facebook is also a very high traffic app; everyone and their grandma uses Facebook. Think about it . . . if you can score a couple of grandma tenants with your listing, you'll have free cookies for life!

Craigslist

Craigslist is another excellent place to find tenants. While it costs $5 to post a listing (and everyone who responds is anonymous), coverage is massive – and you will be giving each applicant a very extensive background check through your vetting process.

Craigslist's high traffic is its greatest selling point, and you know what the great House Hackers of Old say: The more eyeballs, the better!

Zillow

To list your room on a platform that pretty much organizes your listing and shows it to the right people, consider Zillow. You can pay as little as $10 per week, which is backed by a lead guarantee. That means no leads, no charge. Zillow also posts your listing on other third-party websites, like Trulia and Hotpads.

Zillow is expensive, but it does get your listing in front of a lot of people. So, if Facebook and Craigslist are duds, then try Zillow.

Spare Room and other apps

Spare room and other apps like this are less known and have some of the lowest quality leads. But desperate times call for desperate measures. Posting the same listing you crafted for Facebook MarketPlace on SpareRoom is another cheap way to pick up more eyeballs.

Realtor

If you really can't find someone, then you can hire a realtor to find a renter for your home. It is, by far, the most expensive option; I usually skip it unless my room has been vacant for more than a month.

Airbnb

Airbnb is another excellent way to rent out a spare room or an extra area in your home. For instance, if you only have your living room or an open office, you can put it up on Airbnb. Even if you take subpar photos and write a lousy listing, someone will likely rent it every now and then.

For more details on posting your spare room on Airbnb, you can read my book *No Property No Problem*. But for now, just know that short-term and medium-term rentals are still a great way for you to make money on your spare rooms, and Airbnb is perhaps one of the safest ways to rent out a room thanks to their two-way review system. (You get to see reviews of your guests before you give them the go-ahead to rent.)

You may not know it, but Airbnb offers medium-stay renting, where you rent an area for a period of between one and six months. They'd still sign a lease, but you'd find them through Airbnb, and their rental period wouldn't be for long.

Depending on who you are, renting in the short or medium-term might be a downside. Some people don't like change; a new tenant every month might set off your "stranger-danger" alarm. But it's another great place to find a tenant for those awkward spaces in your home that could kind-of-act-as-a-room – but not for any reasonable long-term renter.

If you go this route, you must stage whichever room you will be renting on Airbnb, providing an addendum in your other tenant's leases stating that short-term rentals are being considered. Yes, it's your house, and you can do what you want with it, but it's courteous to let your tenants know there will be an Airbnb guest there - especially on a short-term basis. Remember: the more considerate you are to your tenants, the longer they'll stay.

FurnishedFinder.com and other apps

FurnishedFinder is an app similar to Airbnb, but it specifically caters to traveling nurses and other medical professionals. You need to pay a small fee to be listed on their platform, and your rooms will need to be furnished, but it's a great tool to help hack your house. You'll know these tenants are professionals, quiet, and each is only there for a few months. If you don't like them, you just have to wait a little while, and the problem will resolve itself.

Plus, this is a great way to *practice selecting roommates*. It's like speed running the last ten years of my life, as far as selecting tenants goes.

First Impressions Are Everything... Especially For a Listing!

It's believed that – on average – you compete with 100 other rental properties when you advertise your unit online (Jankelow, 2020). The numbers could be even higher, depending on the neighborhood you live in or when you post your listing (like during peak seasons).

When there's such a high demand for affordable accommodations, a prospective tenant will only spend an average of three seconds looking at your listing before deciding to either continue reading or move to the next one. Moral: You have only three seconds to make a good impression!

Since the decision is usually made rapidly, focus on drawing as much attention to your listing as possible. You can do this by nailing these three factors: the headline, the description, and the flagship photo.

Writing a Catchy Headline

The headline is the first chance you have to win the prospective tenant over. This, along with your picture, is the only thing they'll have to decide if they want to dive further into your listing.

If your headline doesn't indicate what a tenant can expect from the rental, the tenant may assume that your rental is not "the one." The best headlines are usually very straightforward, showing the prospective tenant precisely what your rental offers. Don't exaggerate what you're offering in the headline because you'll have a whole lot of explaining to do if they discover you lied.

The #1 goal for your headline: make your prospective tenant *open the listing.* That's it. You're just trying to generate some interest.

Your headline should accurately describe what kind of room your tenant will get and include something that could interest them. Need some examples? Open up Facebook Marketplace and peruse the current inventory. I always search for "room rental."

This *competitor analysis* is not as important for house hacking. Still, if you wanted to set up other real estate streams of income (like Airbnb or start a passive income business like 3-D printing), then it would be extra important!

The first thing you'll notice when you look at Facebook Marketplace is that you only get 20 characters to make your point. The second thing you'll see is that everyone wastes those 20 characters with "Room for Rent..." *At least, they do in my area!*

The next most popular thing you see is something like "Private Bedroom."

This is better, getting closer to being specific and attractive – but it's also what everyone *expects*. Why waste your precious 20 characters on describing the bare minimum?

If you click on a listing, it will bring you to the actual listing. Those of you with a keen eye will see that the title is *longer than 20 characters.*

What does this mean?

People who are good at advertising know this means you put the most exciting part first. It still needs to relate to renting out one room because that's what we're doing. However, it needs to capitalize on the 20 characters you have. If it generates enough targeted interest, then your prospect will click into your ad and read the rest of the title.

Get in the minds of your prospective tenant. What would *you* be looking for if you were trying to rent? And what does your house have that prospective renters would love?

Does this room have a private bed *and* bathroom? Then maybe you want to say

Private bed & bath . . .

. . . because that might not be typical for your area.

Is your house in a sought-after part of town? For Austin, it's West Campus; if I had a house in West Campus, then I would advertise that.

West Campus Room (private) is how I'd likely start my listing; this also affects SEO and how Marketplace lists things. I won't go into it, but it's a good idea to put the location first as long as there aren't ten other Marketplace posts with that exact location.

Is your house new? Do you have a hot tub?

Private Bed [HOT TUB]

There are a million different things you can do to attract people to your listing with your title. But the front end of your title needs to be optimized to attract people's attention.

If you have an extra character, putting one emoji in front is an eye-catching trick.

Some winning emojis are…

💧 🔥 💢 ❗ 💬 (for girls) 🤓 😐 🤯 (for students) 🧑‍🎓

You might not be a natural at this at first, but that's ok. You live and learn! And you can always change your listing.

The rest of your title should have other tantalizing things. Like

Close to Major highway!

Minutes away from the company campus!

Campus bus route!

Make those characters count.

A complete example would look something like this:

> 🔥 Private Bed&Bath|HOT TUB|On Campus Bus Route 🚌

Notice how this title is not written using excellent English? It doesn't even have a space between bed & bath! But your prospective tenants won't care. They just care about what they will get out of their new room. The more things you can put in your title to attract their attention, the more they'll want to click on your listing - which is the whole point!

Seal the Deal With Stunning Photos

Back to our Facebook Marketplace competitor analysis! The front of the listing comprises three components: Title (nailed that!), the price (we know that from earlier), and the picture.

Words can only tell so much of the story; photos seal the deal! And your first photo is the one going to make your prospective tenants click on your listing. So, it needs to meet a few criteria.

Quality. All of your photos must be quality photos. When someone looks at your listing, they will probably flip through a few images; when they are *seriously* considering contacting you, they will look at *all* of your photos. So, you need to make sure they're all quality –more on that in a second.

Unique. That first photo needs to be something unique, something the other listings don't have – like your hot tub, a gorgeous view, a picture of a nearby park, etc. To determine what is unique, you need to look at what your competitors are showing. Are they all showing the bedroom? Are they all showing the kitchen? Is it usually the front door? Whatever most of them show, either make sure your picture looks better than theirs – or *show something else*.

Eye-catching. The uniqueness factor will do a lot to make the photo eye-catching. But designing your room well and color-correcting the shot will do the rest. If you've decided to take a bedroom picture, don't just take a picture of an empty room and stick it there as your first photo. Make sure the room is decorated and furnished! Or better yet, use a different image. (*You can include these bare rooms in the rest of your pictures, but who's going to be interested in a listing with an empty room when there's another listing showing what that room could look like, right below it?*) For color correcting, you can pay any level-two seller on Fiver.com $1 per photo for color-correcting; it's worth it, so do it!

Related. One time, I tried to advertise my listing with a free photo from Pixabay. It was a photo of a dog winking. It was cute, and a lot of people saw it, but unfortunately, it didn't get that many hits. You need to make sure your photo is related to the room you're trying to rent.

So, do you know what you want to be your flagstone photo? Good! Now, we'll talk about taking the photos. You can take the pictures yourself with your smartphone, but if you prefer a professional, find one using Google. In my area, they cost between $100 and $250. They take the photos, photo-correct, and send you the good ones; they take care of everything!

The good news about taking professional photos is that you only have to do it once. You can use them for every listing for that house . . . forever. Well, at least until the design patterns change enough for your potential renters to notice.

If you want to DIY them, you can take good pictures. You not only have the ability, but it's also easy! Here is an excerpt from my book *Beach House Business Model,* which describes how to take pictures for your Airbnb listing. Good photos are good photos, whether you're posting them on Facebook, Craigslist, or Airbnb.

- **Clean!** If you don't have the time to clean, hire a maid service to come in and do a thorough job. Pay attention to detail when you clean because any grease or stain can be easily seen in a picture. For example, clean your stovetops, deep-clean your carpets, and ensure there are no watermarks on surfaces because those show up – sometimes looking strange - on your pictures.

- **Take time to stage the room.** Beautiful staging can elevate the quality and appeal of a picture. If you need ideas on how to stage your room, then look at how other Airbnb investors in your area are staging theirs. Your photographer might help you, but that generally isn't in their job description.

- **Know what pictures you want.** When taking pictures for Airbnb, you want four for each bedroom (from each corner), one per bathroom, and two for every other room. You also want a nice photo of the front and back of the house – and the yard. Make sure the photographer knows this, so they add the photos you need for your packet.

If you'd rather not use a professional photographer, I have a few tips to help you take very professional-looking photos. The great news is that you can use any modern smartphone to take stunning pictures. Most newer phones even have necessary editing features within the camera or photos app. So, if you have a smartphone, put it to use by taking your own pictures! Do everything you would do *if a professional were coming* (clean, stage, and decide on which pictures you want) and consider the following tips.

How to Hold Your Phone

Hold your phone horizontally (landscape) and at hip level. Have your flash turned off (but all room lights turned on and all blinds or curtains open). Have the grid view and HDR turned on — this can be found in your settings. Last, tap on the screen before shooting so your photos are in focus!

***Literally*, Take 100 Pictures**

As a novice photographer, you probably won't take a perfect picture every time. So, the more you take, the more likely you will find excellent ones! When you sit down to look at your photos later, you'll be able to tell which ones great and which ones are just okay.

Editing Your Pictures

Selection

If you are like me and have trouble deciding, pick too many for your first round and whittle it down in subsequent rounds. Get some fresh eyes on the pictures. People might not know how to take great photos, but they'll know good ones when they see them!

Editing

You will most likely need to export your photos to some editing app – and many come standard with every computer. Find yours or go online and find a free one to get started. If you're absolutely terrible at this, you can go on Fiverr.com and pay someone to do this for you. It will probably cost you $1 per photo. Just search for "Real Estate Photo Editing."

To do this yourself, here are a few tips:

- Adjust the brightness so your photos are bright. Make sure whatever your focus is on is the brightest. Don't go too far and make it look like it's a painting, but brighten that place up! One way you can do this is to turn up the blue saturation in your photos. There's something about seeing blue that makes humans feel light and fuzzy on the inside.

- Make sure the pictures are straight! Find something that was straight and straighten the photo based on that. It could be a tall lamp, a corner, or a door. Whatever it is, make your photo straight.

- Make sure nothing is glaring at you - no shiny bright spots.

- If your photos have points that are too bright, then adjust your highlight. You want a good balance between light and dark.

- Crop your photos to a 2:3 baseline - it's what Airbnb uses.

Once you have the photos you like ready to go, it's time to put them on your listing.

That's the end of that excerpt! I'll close this chapter with a few examples of quality photos I would include in my house hacking listing.

How to Live for Free

Short and Sweet Descriptions

Your title and flagship picture are what will attract your potential tenant. Your description is what seals the deal. Once people click on your listing, it's go-time. Imagine Carl sitting in his car, drinking his latte, reading your description, and judging you based on your listing. If he likes what he sees from the picture and title, he'll tap on it and get moved into your description.

But this just buys you another three seconds. People do not have long attention spans, so don't write *A History of my Property* on Facebook Marketplace. You can tell them that later when showing your house.

Start by describing the A-minus features. Your A+ features should be in your description, and since it's Facebook Marketplace, they probably just read them in your title anyway. There's no point in re-writing them.

Try avoiding common phrases, like "convenient location" or "spacious bedroom," because many listings online are littered with those! Instead, try to help prospective tenants visualize the experience of living in your rental. Check out this example below:

~~~~~~~~~~

Automated Retirees

Freshly renovated, modern 1-bedroom, 1-bath guest house in a vibrant suburb.

Spend the day at amazing coffee shops ☕ and restaurants [within walking distance!], or clear your mind in one of the many parks. 🌳

Perfect for the young professional looking for a calm and stress-free environment.

🐾 Pets allowed!

We will accept a 6 or 12-month lease. $750/month, 1-month security deposit. Utilities not included. Call Cat at 888-8888.

~~~~~~~~~

Here's another example:

~~~~~~~~~

🛏 Private Bed&Bath[Fully Furnished!]

One room with a private bathroom available for sublet in a 2-bed/2-bath apartment in west campus.

🏙 5 Minutes from downtown!

The room is fully furnished, and the apartment has all appliances, including a washer/dryer, a stovetop, and a fridge. Internet and cable are included in the rent as well!

Vaping in the apartment is fine, but there's a designated area on the balcony for smokers.

Contact me for more info if interested. We will accept a 6- or 12-month lease. $750/month, 1-month security deposit. Utilities not included. Call Cat at 888-8888.

~~~~~~~~~

I like using emojis in my listing because they catch people's eyes and help highlight the positives. If someone isn't going to read my whole listing, they'll probably still read the stuff around the emojis.

You'll also notice I put a lot of line breaks in my listings. People don't like reading huge blocks of text. Especially if they're just trying to glean the main points of whatever they're reading. Imagine if this book was just one massive block of text with no line breaks. I bet you'd hate reading it. I bet you wouldn't even finish it! It would be such a monumental task you might even go right ahead and burn this book, ashamed that anyone who was also a fellow human would write a book formatted so horribly. But believe it or not, there's something even worse than writing a huge block of text in a book . . . writing a listing formatted as one continuous block of text. No one wants to read a listing formatting like that! At this point, I'm sure you see that I'm just trying to make this paragraph one huge block of text to prove a point. I bet if you're reading this book, you won't even make it to the bottom of this paragraph. You'll probably just skip it and move right on to the next one! Or if you did make it down here, you made it down here because you skipped the rest and just read the bottom of the paragraph. Oh, now that I've said that, you will try to reread it. I know I would! But then again, I'm pretty nosy. At any rate, if you did read that whole thing, well done! Don't make your listings blocks of text. And if you do, at least try to make them funny.

As a house hacker posting a simple listing on Facebook once or twice, it isn't paramount that your listing be perfect. After all, you're not reselling the same room 15 times a month to make money on Airbnb. You're just selling a few rooms in your house once a year.

So, no matter how terrible you think your listing is, you need to post it. It will eventually generate enough interest. Don't worry if you can't do all the things I've mentioned in the listing section. Just try to do as many of them as you can because the sooner you find tenants, the sooner you make money!

Finding The Diamond in the Rough

As mentioned earlier, post your listing in as many places as possible. Selling is a numbers game. If 200 people see your listing, maybe two will call you. That's a 1% success rate. That same success rate turns into 20 people if you show it to 2000 people! And that's a good thing because you want to be selective with your tenants.

Screening a contact doesn't begin when they are ready to sign a lease agreement. The process starts the moment you receive your first call. Even though it's usually a phone conversation, you can decipher a lot of key info from a 5-minute chat.

I like to glean the following from any prospective tenant in the first conversation. . .

Occupation

For me, all that matters is that they have a stable job. If you would prefer that everyone work during the day instead of at night (like nighttime emergency room nurses, paramedics, etc.), consider when speaking to them.

After living with a variety of tenants throughout the years, I find that nighttime workers are a joy to live with. They use the kitchen when you'd be asleep (and vice versa). So, if no one lives near the kitchen, then it's perfect! This might be different if your room is right outside the kitchen or if you've used the living room as your Master. So, make sure you make this decision with your floor plan in mind.

One thing that does matter is how much they make. They DO need to make three times what they will spend in rent each month to be considered a "safe" candidate. That's just a general rule. If they earn a little less, then it's probably okay. For instance, if you charge $500 per month, they need to make at least $1500 per month (before taxes) to qualify for your room.

Since you're vetting them in this phone call, they will expect you to ask them questions like that – don't feel like you're asking rude or nosy questions.

Pets

Are you willing to allow pets on your property? If so, what kind of pets will you allow, and will your tenant pay an extra fee to have their pets live with them?

Dogs and cats can cause a lot of wear on the house. From accidents on the carpet to creating an odor that seeps into the paint to absolutely destroying a door from chewing on it . . . animals can cause damage. Even tanked animals, like fish!

Can you imagine your heart rate when you hear 30 gallons of water gracefully spewing out of a fish tank? It doesn't feel good, that's for sure! If you already have pets or have a house with older carpets, then allowing pets probably isn't that big of a deal. After all, going from zero dogs to one is a much bigger deal than going from one dog to five. But be aware, a poorly trained dog can destroy your house.

Let me tell you two stories to illustrate my point.

My neighbors are amazing people. They foster dogs from a company called Austin Pets Alive! – a no-kill nonprofit animal shelter. The shelter had a dog (abandoned by his owners) with cancer, and they decided to foster "Tank," giving him as good of a life as possible (he didn't have long to live . . . who wants to spend their last days living in a cage?)

One night, my neighbors went out to eat, and in their absence, Tank proceeded to destroy parts of their home; he ate half a door, demolished their couch, and almost broke a window. While this is a very extreme case, it can happen to your house if you allow pets.

Remember Mr. and Mrs. T from the beginning? They also allowed pets in their home. They already had some pets (several dogs and cats, and even a few snakes), so they figured it was no big deal – nothing has happened to their house, outside of the usual accident now and then.

Like earlier (when we discussed cleanliness tolerances), people have a pet tolerance too. Some people don't care if their animals don't make it outside. Other people believe that training their animals is immoral. When you allow pets in your home, you are taking this chance.

I've never allowed pets in all my time renting rooms; you don't have to either. But if you do, it opens you up to more tenants and can even increase your cash flow by a few hundred bucks each month.

Smokers

Do you allow smoking in the house, or is there a designated area for smokers? Do you care if your tenants vape in the house?

For me, smoking (tobacco) and vaping are two different things. Smoking – especially controlled substances like marijuana – is a big no-no for anyone who wants to live in my house. They can use the patio if they'd like. There's even a convenient ashtray outside, just for them.

This is a problem for people who chain smoke. I don't care if they choose to move on to smokier pastures because they *cannot* smoke in my house. The smell of smoke ruins houses, and it's hard to rid your home of that particular odor.

To do so, you must repaint, recarpet, and use an ozone machine. Even then, often, you can *still* smell the residual tobacco. I'm not into that, especially for some random tenant that likely will only be with me for a year. So, generally, I say no to smokers.

Vaping, on the other hand, doesn't leave a smell. I don't necessarily like it, but it doesn't damage the house, and I don't believe it will harm me, so I allow it.

Make that distinction for yourself but remember: if you allow vaping, you might have to let your other tenants know it. Check your state's laws for clarification on that.

Gender

Are you a single woman who would prefer all ladies? Or a guy who wants to avoid the whole *New Girls* situation? Do you even care?

Typically, it is illegal to expressly limit which gender may live in your rentals. However, when you share living spaces, you get an exemption. Here's an excerpt straight from HUD.

Federal Fair Housing laws prohibit discriminatory advertising in all housing, regardless of how large or small the property. ***However, advertising which expresses a preference based upon sex is allowed in shared living situations where tenants will share a bathroom, kitchen, or other common area****. [emphasis added]*

So, since you'll live with them, you get the right to say *no* based on gender. You can even include it in your ad!

Hobbies

Ok, I'll say it. Some hobbies are more annoying than others. I've had tenants who play video games as a hobby. As long as your walls aren't too thin and they don't decide to take up residence in a shared space, this is the best hobby a roommate could have! Well, besides knitting.

Because . . . others like to party. If they like to party, you can be sure that party will come back to your house sometimes. And sure, if it's just now and then or you have a big house, who cares?! But if it's every weekend, right outside your room . . . that's an issue.

Instruments can also be a big deal. You need to make sure they either play a quiet instrument or can make their loud instrument quiet. If they can't quiet it down, you still have a few options.

First, you can tell them they can't practice when they live with you; this will cause most to seek greener pastures. Second, you can make a deal with them: they can only play when no one else is home. That might also cause some issues. What if other people are always home? What if you're usually not home, and then a pandemic occurs – keeping everyone home all the time? What then?

You also have your other tenants to think of. Maybe you're fine with a light drum serenade every day at 5:00 pm, but they probably aren't. As the owner, it's up to you to make sure everyone has a great experience. Unfortunately, that's difficult when one of your tenants has a loud hobby the others aren't into.

Now that you've had a little bit of time considering who you want to rent to, let's get to screening!

Step 1: Call Every Person Who Responded to Your Listing

These phone calls shouldn't take hours; you need only to make a formal introduction, tell them a little about yourself, and then ask about them.

Try to have a natural, easygoing conversation but learn as much as you can about them at the same time. The conversation shouldn't last over five minutes and should include gathering the following information:

- What do they do for a living?
- Do they have any pets or kids?
- When are they available for a showing?
- Will they be bringing furniture, or will they need furniture?
- Are they okay with paying the fees for a background check?
- What are some of their hobbies? Are their hobbies loud? Do they like to party? You want to screen for negative traits that could cause issues with the other tenants.

- Would they mind providing two character witnesses and four years of past landlord history?

If you liked talking to them on the phone, then you can move on to the next step.

Step 2: Call Past Landlords and Character Witnesses

Calling past landlords is a bit of a gamble. Some landlords will tell you everything you want to know, and others won't even return your calls. If you can, ask the previous landlords about their history with the renter, whether they gave them any trouble, and how they treated their property. Sometimes, you will find that current landlords will lie to get a bad tenant out of their home (landlords from two rentals ago are more likely to share red flags).

The reason for calling character witnesses is similar to why you need to contact previous landlords, except the character witnesses are even more likely to lie to you because they want to help their friends! But . . . *they're worse at it*. They don't know what you want to hear in most cases and might even lie to their friend's detriment! Here are some of my favorites sleuthing questions:

- How long have you known your friend?
- Do they play any instruments or enjoy any hobbies?

- Does your friend like to party?
- Does your friend have any pets?
- Why is your friend interested in this city or looking for a place to rent?

Of course, as they answer each question, you can ask them follow-ups to clarify. I've asked as many as ten follow-up questions, catching many "good friends" in a lie or story that didn't match up with what the tenant told me earlier.

Step 3: Perform a Credit Score and Background Check

There are a ton of online services that will perform a background and credit score check for you; you have only to search for them. To search, type "Background check <city> tenant".

With credit scores, 680 is usually as low as I will go unless the renter is right out of college or high school. Kids that age might not have a credit score, so it's really not a great indication of who they are. Those guys are usually great candidates for having their parents cosign. Then I can check *their parent's credit scores.*

You will want to look at the prospective tenant's work history as well. I only rent to tenants who have had a steady job for at least the past year . . . or a good reason to have taken a gap year. Still, they must have had a steady job sometime in the past few years. Maybe they took a gap year to take care of their mom; *they get a pass*. If they took a gap year to find themselves after a string of twelve-week long jobs . . . uh, no.

I also check criminal records. Speeding tickets are one thing, but it's a pass from me if they have a serious criminal history. We're trying to avoid areas with crime, not take it with us!

Another critical metric is evictions. If they were evicted before, they'd likely be okay with another one. You don't want someone who doesn't mind evictions; that means they're also fine not paying!

Hopefully, the process of screening your tenants will rule a lot out. You should be left with exactly the number of tenants you need, plus a few backups. If they all accept, then it's time to set a move-in date and sign a lease!

For creating rental contracts, I'm a fan of [Rocket Lawyer](). This online legal software can create a lease contract specific to your state and additional provisions for only $30. There's no way of getting around the contract — you must have one – even if you're renting to a family member or a friend. Don't try to cheap out on it, either; $30 for an ironclad contract is worth it.

There's also the matter of the deposit – I always ask for the first and last month's rent as a deposit. If they have a dog, cat, or a fish, I make them give me two extra months' rent as well. That's typical for deposits where I live, but your market might be different. The best way to find out is to look at other listings in your area.

The deposit serves as a kind of insurance if the tenant destroys something. For instance, if they put a hole in the wall, break your microwave, or stain your carpet, you can keep part or all of their deposit.

You might think that you'll just charge them exactly what the repair costs, but that amounts to whatever *you think is fair* for the repair. One time, I was charged a $300 moving fee for leaving a broken hose in the backyard and a $200 cleaning fee for leaving the oven door dirty! *Deposits are a racket!*

If the deposit doesn't cover what they broke, you can ask them for more money to cover the damages or sue them. Often, suing tenants costs you more money and time than it's worth, so I wouldn't recommend it unless they burn down your house.

However, if you do your due diligence initially, finding people that seem reliable, then you should be fine. The deposit is not to cover things like a broken water heater, a broken roof, minor wear-and-tear; it's designed to cover what the *tenant broke.* If the water heater broke while they were using the shower, you can't charge them for the cost of a new water heater.

However, if they hammered a nail into the water heater and caused it to leak (who would do that?!), you can charge them for a replacement (and likely the installation charges!) Extensive repairs and maintenance costs are part of being a homeowner. You could live only in the entryway of your home and use the hose nozzle outside to shower… and something would still break in your house. That's why we factored in 10%-15% of our rent towards an *Operating Fund* earlier, making sure we had either three months' rent or at least $5,000!

TL;DR

The perfect tenant? It all boils down to how compatible they are with your lifestyle (remember that your tenants must integrate into your life and not the other way around). The internet is a great resource for finding suitable tenants. Distribute your listing to as many free and cheap platforms as possible so you can collect those eyeballs!

Your listing is what attracts them to your property! When designing it, you must focus on three main factors: the headline, description, and photos. Remember that you don't have a lot of time to convince prospective tenants that your rental is perfect for them, so use your words and photos wisely!

Once you've got a few people interested, you will pick the best ones by screening them. The screening process begins from the very first phone call you have with your prospective tenants. Listen more than you speak, gathering as much information as you can about the kind of people they are.

Part 3

Living Large and In Charge

CHAPTER 5

How to Live With Tenants—Peacefully

The happiness of your life depends on the quality of your thoughts.

— Marcus Aurelius

What You Can Expect From This Chapter

- Why rules will save you when nothing else can
- How to become a Landmate <3
- How to have those discussions you really don't want to have
- The top five mistakes new landlords have and how to avoid them

"Peace" Is The Operative Word Here

When I was growing up, we'd wake up every Saturday and scrub the house. And I mean, we'd scrub that house. It would be immaculately clean by the time we were done. And you know what? I'm pretty proud of that. I can clean a toilet like nobody's business – thanks to my parents.

I've had a variety of roommates over the years; I am a much better roommate now for it because *I get it*. No matter how careful you are in vetting or how long you've known the person, problems happen. Every human is different. Not everyone's parents made them wake up on Saturday and clean. Actually, that's kind of a dying art nowadays, as far as I know.

My first flatmate was the person I had roomed with in the dorms the year before. Let's call her Carly.

Carly was a nice girl whose parents didn't teach her how to clean – and she *wouldn't* clean. *Anything!* It would bug the crap out of me, but I never told her. I just suffered through it and quietly wondered why she had such terrible parents.

She and I had had no problems living in the dorms together because the dorms had a maid who cleaned the bathroom — and sweeping a 15 x 15 room? Pshh . . . that only took ten minutes anyway, so who cares?

But when we lived in a 2-bedroom apartment with its own kitchen and un-maided bathroom, well, that was a problem. And to me, it wasn't a *small* problem; it was like the end of the world!

Carly and I had started the year as good friends, but by the end of the year, we rarely even spoke . . . even though we lived together. We parted ways, and I'm pretty sure she was so upset that she even unfriended me on Facebook.

You certainly need not be friends with your tenants, but you should at least strive to be on good terms. What Carly and I did was technically considered living together . . . but I wouldn't describe it as pleasant or peaceful.

No one likes having an awkward conversation. Some of us are more introverted than others and will try to avoid it at all costs – but you can't. You need to air your dirty laundry so your roommates can help you clean it.

Luckily, there is a system to avoid some of these issues that arise when you live together – namely, *rules and separation.*

The more separation from your tenants, the better. It doesn't matter if they are your best friend or a stranger – everyone needs their own space. In my house, we all know which spaces are private and which are shared. Ed and I have our bedroom, our office, and the garage all to ourselves. (He LOVES working on cars!)

My tenants have their bedroom, their office, and the upstairs game room.

The kitchen, my gym, and the downstairs living room is shared space. So, if any of us want to be alone or away from each other, we know where to go!

My in-laws also both work at night, so Ed and I have free reign over the house most of the day (and most nights). This is a perfect arrangement for us because we never have to fight over who is using the kitchen or the laundry room as our schedules are completely opposite.

However, it's best to talk with your tenants about your expectations and needs. For instance, they could have the entire upstairs, and you could have the entire downstairs.

The best way to lay this out is by having them read and sign a rulebook when they sign their lease. If the rules are laid out to them from the first day, it will be less awkward for you to tell them they're breaking one of them. But here's the deal; you also need to follow your own rules. You're entering into an agreement between them and yourself – and agreements work best when they are fair and equal.

Rules Aren't For Suckers

If you're open to the idea of renting out a room in your house, you'll likely have some expectations about how tenants should behave in your living space. You cannot assume that every tenant will automatically share the same ideas and beliefs as you. Thus, it's always recommended to draft a rule book that sets clear parameters of the kinds of behaviors that are acceptable and unacceptable in your home. There are three reasons why establishing house rules can benefit you as the property owner:

1. House rules communicate what you may be too afraid or uncomfortable to communicate yourself. They will get to know where you stand on a few issues and how you expect life in your home to flow.
2. When rules have been put on paper, signed, and discussed, tenants are less likely to violate them (*especially if it could result in their eviction*).
3. House rules also allow you to take legal action when tenants have violated your rules or caused damage to your property.

There is no rule book for creating a rule book (excuse the pun), but here are the basic rules I've gathered over the years.

Rules About Tenants' Right of Entry

I like for each tenant to have their own entry code. That way, I need not replace the locks every time someone wants to move out; I just delete their code.

One rule about those codes: they *cannot* share their code with any tenant or any of their family or friends. Only tenants can have codes, and only those tenants should know their own code.

No exceptions.

If they want to include a significant other, that person can have their own code. And I am the only one who can create and delete codes.

There may also be places in your home that are off-limits. Do you have a room with a safe and other valuables? Maybe your mother occupies a certain part of the house; that is her space that no one is allowed in. Whatever the case, ensure those limits are crystal clear in the rules.

Rules About Garbage Removal, Upkeep, and Gardening

It's vital to set rules regarding the home's upkeep so your property may retain its value. Consider some rules about cleanliness, the removal of garbage, recycling, and keeping the rooms livable.

For gardening and cleaning, a professional service can work wonders. I'd even suggest passing along the costs to your tenants – or at least their fair share.

But, if you want to cheap out and set up a chore schedule, then make sure it's in the rules. When I was in college, we cleaned, gardened, and did our own shopping; I just couldn't afford to hire a maid service or gardener once a month.

Nowadays, I try to build it into my monthly rent. It's just so much easier to charge $50 extra a month and be done with the landscaping and cleaning. At least then I know it'll get done – and it'll be done right. As for trash, dishes, and other things we talked about in the cleanliness section, make sure you have it all spelled out in the rulebook.

Rules About Quiet Hours and General Noise

How loud can your residents be? And *when*? If you live in a neighborhood, then it's likely you already have quiet hours that you must adhere to. Usually, it's from 10 pm to 6 am. However, it might also be a good idea to set quiet hours for your house as well. I've even had to regulate volume levels on the television; anyone watching TV in the living room cannot have the volume above 15 after 10 pm. (Yes, that's actually in my rulebook.)

This also gives you and your tenants the freedom to throw parties but restricts how loud they can be past certain hours as a courtesy to everyone else in the house. Of course, if everyone in the house is invited, you might break those rules a little bit!

Rules About the Appropriate Use of Shared Spaces

Typically, your tenants will congregate in three spaces: the bathroom, kitchen, and living room. Since these common areas will be used frequently, it's essential to ensure that your tenants know how to behave in those spaces and how to properly use the technology or appliances placed there.

For example, provide directives on what can and cannot be flushed down the toilet, how to switch kitchen appliances on and off, and when old food should be cleaned out of the refrigerator. You have no idea how many expired containers and moldy fruit I've thrown away over the years. Yuck! Some of my tenants even got upset – thus, the rule. If it's expired, it's going in the trash. *No exceptions.*

Rules About Guests

We talked about this earlier on, so I won't repeat myself. Still, make sure you have some rules about guests, Tinder dates, and long-term significant others in the rule book. You need something to point to if your tenants do things you don't like, are dangerous, or are annoying your other tenants.

Treat Everyone Kindly And Respect Everyone's Personal Space

Since you have multiple strangers staying in the same house, this needs to be explicitly stated. This rule should cover everything from calling another tenant names to trespassing in someone else's room to physical assault.

So, what happens when tenants violate your house rules? Foremost, the procedure you follow for addressing violations must be written down and explained to tenants at the beginning of their rental term. Some violations, such as playing music too loud, can usually be taken care of with a text.

Other violations might be cause for legal action. Violations like assault, abuse of another tenant, theft, or any other security or safety breach are serious violations of not only your rules but the law.

It's up to you on how you want to handle violations; however, I highly recommend that you enforce the rules evenly and fairly. Follow the consequences you set on your rule book and make sure your tenants are held accountable for bad behavior.

If you need to get the law involved, do it as quickly as possible. Thankfully, I've never had to call the police in all the time I've been house hacking. This is typical for landlords that vet their tenants for crime initially – so take due diligence seriously!

Most of these problems take care of themselves as long as you have quality tenants.

How to Be a Landmate

You're not just a landlord; you're their housemate. How can you be both? Especially to strangers . . . especially to friends.

Looking at it from the landlord's perspective, living in your own home while having tenants occupy unused spaces is a neat way to pay off your property. It also allows you to keep a close eye on your property and act fast when they break something.

But, looking at it as a roommate, sometimes these people can get on your *last nerve!* What if you're trying to watch TV while they're playfully cooking pasta? What if you want to do something loud, like have your roof fixed, while they're asleep?

It's a whole lot easier to live alone in your own house – without roommates. And when you do have roommates, you want to be their friend. After all, you live with these people; you can't communicate solely through business documents with a side of cold shoulder.

How do you reconcile these two ideas?

The answer is communication! Communicate early and often. Build your rule book and enforce the rules! Communication goes both ways, though. Your tenants need to feel free to talk to you openly and honestly about what's bothering them. Communication is key crucial to any successful relationship, especially one that involves money and living together.

A tenant is a client, but it sure makes it easier when they're also a friend. Strive to have a good relationship with the people you live with. You don't want to feel like you have to sleep with one eye open; your house is – and should always be – your sanctuary!

Still, your tenant is a person, too, and you can't treat them like they're a robot. Since you're living with them, you're going to talk to them, get to know them, and understand what struggles they're going through in life. That can make it difficult when they're unable to pay their rent, and you must start taking steps to evict them - especially if they're honest and good at heart.

Real estate isn't just a business; it's also about people. As a house hacker, you are physically dealing with the people your business is helping every day, in person. Because of this, it gives you the freedom to do as much or as little as you want for them.

Once, a lady staying at Mr. and Mrs. T's house was out of a job, living paycheck to paycheck. Many people do. When she lost her job, she couldn't even afford to eat, let alone pay her rent.

Mr. and Mrs. T just couldn't morally put her out on the street, so they came up with another plan. She could stay if she cleaned the house, mowed the lawn twice a month, and was actively searching for work. While this came nowhere close to paying for her rent, it was more than *nothing*. They took a loss that month, but when that woman found work again, she paid them back. And she was a tenant of theirs for a long time after that with absolutely no other problems.

They even taught her how to budget and live below her means. Win/win.

Once, I was renting to a boy named Jim. He'd come from a small town out in the sticks and was trying to make his way in *the big city*. He didn't like the lack of opportunity where he came from. He had nothing when he got to our house, not even a bed (and he couldn't afford to buy one.) He was literally risking everything to make his life better.

Eddy and I bought a cheap mattress from Sam's for him. At that time, we were very poor, but it was only $100, and we could afford that. We also deferred his rent.

It wasn't much, but at least he had something to sleep on!

You can't just treat your clients like robots; you must treat them with empathy. That goes for any business, not just house hacking. (*House hacking just makes it easier to do because you can be their friend to whatever extent you feel comfortable.*)

Rules give you something to fall back on if needed. They exist to provide a legal reason to make your tenants do something for the good or safety of the household. That said, you need to be there for them, too.

Do your best to be a human who happens to collect checks from their friends and takes their concerns seriously. That's how you become a great landmate.

The Introvert's Guide to Hard Discussions

Before you say it, *I know.* Extroverts can have a hard time discussing issues too! It's just that we introverts have it even worse than you. We don't even like *talking* to people, let alone *confronting* them! Especially people we have to see all the time. Talk about impossible . . .

But it has to be done. Contrary to many people's beliefs, you don't have to be a monster to get your point across. You can be gentle but firm.

I grew up around a lot of boisterous Italians. Believe me, if they had a problem with you, they would tell you, no matter who was around or what you were doing. So, I grew up hating confrontation because it seemed so *verbally violent* every time it happened.

My mom isn't Italian. She grew up in a quiet, happy family that liked to handle things by talking about them calmly. Naturally, her conflict resolution style is not one I even noticed growing up because it happened so quietly and seamlessly.

She'd creep into your room, talk to you about anything and everything and then, eventually, slip it in. "So, you know something I've been thinking about? It would be pretty nice to set a schedule for who takes the garbage out to the street. Don't you think?"

Easy, seamless, and effective.

She'd get her way without even breaking a sweat. She was diplomatic yet firm. And that's precisely how you need to be as a landmate. Try creating a win-win situation with every issue you need to solve. If someone broke the rules, no big deal. Just have a little chat with them. They didn't do it to hurt you personally– they probably weren't thinking about you at all!

However, sometimes a little tough love and boisterous argument is needed. No matter how hard you try, sometimes people don't get it. You could have had a diplomatic conversation with them four, five, twenty times. At that point, they're either doing it to spite you or to take advantage of you.

If diplomacy and patience don't work, then you need to get loud. Thankfully, diplomacy works on 99% of tenants. After all, most people just want to live and be left alone.

Let's talk about how I handle three of the most common problems landmates face with their tenants.

Problem 1: Your Tenant Has Caused Damages to Your Property

For whatever reason, a tenant damaging my property is almost like a spiritual experience for me . . . a *negative* one. I have to fight against my natural reaction to take it personally. How could they – *why could they* – damage stuff that I worked hard for and strived to maintain?

Most times, it's an honest mistake, and the tenant is more than happy to pay for it with some money out of their deposit. Usually, it's obvious who broke what, so it's not an issue. Besides, as we talked about earlier, it's tax-deductible anyway.

Sometimes, the tenant refuses to take responsibility. This is where conflict resolution shines. Now it's up to you to get to the bottom of who caused the damage. Once, no one would take responsibility for a dent in my garage door. So, I had a conversation with each of them to get the whole story.

In the end, everyone pitched in a bit of money to have the garage door fixed. The culprit outed herself because she felt guilty. (*I'm not sure why she didn't feel guilty when it was just me paying for it, but that's another story!*)

One of the great things about living with your tenants is inspecting their spaces. A quick peek in their room can tell you the entire story, like when one tenant refused to wear deodorant in his room while he was gaming. And it was noticeable. I caught and handled that one quick enough to stop the lasting damage of man-stank in my paint!

Problem 2: Your Tenant Is Late On Their Rent Payment . . . Again!

I am pretty flexible with my payment schedule. I give each tenant half the month to pay their rent, and they can pay me however they'd like to pay me. A few people have Zelle'd the money, some pay by check, and I even had one guy pay in cash each month (he didn't believe in banks.)

I don't care how my tenants pay me, as long as they do; this is *business* after all.

So, how do you talk to people about rent, and what can you do to get them to pay you? First, if someone begins to take advantage of my *pay-me-whenever* attitude, I remove that privilege. Now, they have three days (and no more) to pay me after the first of the month, or they accrue a late fee. This is entirely up to my discretion; as long as I give them written notice, it can be done at any time.

After this goes into effect, if they pay me late, they get charged a late fee. Imagine that!

Now, if I've had a tenant for a while and they've paid me on time every month since the day they got there, I'll probably give them a little more leniency. Most of the time, I'll ask them why they haven't paid me yet, and it's often because they simply forgot. But sometimes, it's because something major is happening in their life.

I once had a tenant who had to fly back home for an emergency. The plane tickets would cost him the entire month's rent. I'd had *ZERO* problems with this guy up to that point, and no reason to believe he would not pay me back. So, I put him on a payment plan where he paid me $50 a month until the missing rent was paid off.

Most people are so thankful that you've given them these little opportunities that they're never late again – especially if they're already great tenants.

If you accidentally signed a tenant that absolutely won't pay, then that's another story. First, try reminding them. They might give you some excuse or push you off until their next payday. Take them at their word and ask them again (on their payday), or try to set up a payment plan for that *one* time. Make them sign another contract. Do not trust them, especially if they've given you no reason to.

If they don't pay you at the agreed time, then you have two options. Option #1: diplomacy. Try talking to them again. Figure out what's going on; maybe there's some way you can help them. Perhaps there's a deal to be made. Since they're living with you, it would be uncomfortable going through the messy legalities of eviction. (*It's not like you just file paperwork and wham! They're evicted. It's a process that takes time.*)

Option #2: If diplomacy doesn't work, then, unfortunately, eviction is your only option. Out of the dozens of tenants I've had, I have never been forced to evict any of them, so I cannot provide much advice on that front. However, I've avoided evictions by applying all the principles discussed in this book. Properly vetting your tenants and treating them like humans usually works like a charm.

Problem 3: Your Tenant Is Always Complaining About Something

It's part of your job as the landlord to make sure your tenants are happy, right? But what happens when no matter what you do, you cannot seem to please a tenant? They call you at odd hours of the night complaining about the Wi-Fi connection, noisy neighbors, or a creak in the door.

While these may be pressing concerns for them, they aren't legitimate issues worth harassing anyone about, especially not me! So how should landmates handle unreasonable requests or tenants who find pleasure in complaining?

First, it's essential to know your legal rights as a landlord. You are legally obligated to make repairs to the property or fix issues that would make your home inhabitable or unsafe. This doesn't mean you need to attend to every minor issue. For example, the kitchen faucet may be loose and need tightening, but that isn't necessarily a major issue you need to attend to right away – as long as there's clean drinking water coming out of the tap, everybody is good!

Or maybe AT&T told you that you would have *speeds up to 200-Mbps,* but in reality, your roommates love to stream, so you get 33-Mbps most of the month. That's not a serious issue for which they should be waking you up! (*Also, it's against the rule about respect in your rulebook.*)

If one of your tenants likes to complain, then thank them for caring so much about your property and let them know you want all of their complaints in writing. Tell them they should text or email all complaints unless there is a serious medical emergency or a structural issue with the house.

If they continue to bug you at all hours of the day and night, remind them you need their complaints in writing. Let them know they're failing to be respectful of you or the rules, and that might be grounds for legal or monetary repercussions.

Avoid These Five Mistakes That Inexperienced Landlords Make

Becoming a landlord requires more than just buying a house and collecting checks. Here are a few mistakes you should look out for to succeed from the get-go.

Mistake 1: Not Running a Background or Credit Check

Do it. I'm serious.

While there are a few charges associated with background and credit checks, you can make your prospective tenants pay for it. This is money they forfeit to you with their application to live at your house. Where I'm from, it's standard practice.

Most landlords have their prospective tenants pay them via PayPal, Venmo, or Zelle. It usually costs about $50 and is called an *application fee.* Then, they use the application fee on the credit and background checks. You need not give the application fee back, so spend it!

Background checks have helped me avoid a lot of red-flag tenants. Some had assault charges; others were thieves! These people will apply to live with you.

You may be a very trusting person (and we need more people like you in the world), but honestly speaking, your prospective tenant won't tell you the whole truth. Even if your tenant is desperate to move in and can pay three times the deposit cost, don't skip vetting them. I get that everyone has a past, and some people can turn over a new leaf - but don't let your first experience with house hacking be a bad one because you didn't deny criminals the right to stay in your house.

Mistake 2: Thinking That Your Rooms Will Always Be Occupied

When you take out a mortgage on a house, you're likely optimistic that your investment will someday pay itself off. However, the downside to any rental is vacancy.

Sometimes, it can take a month or two to fill a vacancy, especially an unexpected one. Other times, it's no issue. With house hacking, most of your guests will only stay for a year or two, so there is the possibility of your entire house turning over each year. After all, who wants to live in a room forever?

This is why we have our operating fund. It should be able to take care of at least three months of complete vacancy, no matter how unlikely that is. After it's depleted, spend at least half of the rent you get building it back up. Yes, it does cut into your bottom line, but it's more important to have it.

If your lease states that your tenants must give at least a 60-day notice to vacate, then you'll likely never have vacancies. Start advertising your rental immediately after they decide to leave, clarifying that the new tenant can't live there until such-and-such date. Also, give yourself enough time to thoroughly clean the room(s) before a new tenant arrives.

Do yourself a favor and cheat a little: know how dirty your roommate is and budget in enough time to clean. You can use their deposit to hire a one-time deep clean for the room, but maids have a business to run too, and you must get on their schedule.

Mistake 3: Underestimating the Cost of Ongoing Maintenance to the Property

Your tenants are more likely to renew their lease agreement and be comfortable living in your home when it's clean and everything works. Not only that, but you probably don't want to live in a house with a leaky roof, broken water heater, or a giant hole in the driveway where a car could be. Factor in repair costs in the rent so that you're not burdened with bills when it's time to conduct maintenance checks.

That's another reason to keep your operating fund up to snuff.

Mistake 4: Not Making Your Tenants Sign a Lease

Landlords are similar to entrepreneurs, except for us, our business is our home. This means that your tenants are clients who enter into partnership with you and exchange money for a place to live.

It's essential to treat this relationship professionally for your own protection. When tenants fail to meet your rules or expectations, the contract they signed holds them legally accountable. If your agreement was in the form of a simple handshake or promise (this usually happens when landlords rent their units to friends and family) it becomes challenging to hold the tenant accountable for misconduct or failing to make rent payments.

Mistake 5: Raising the Rent Every Year

This rule may not apply to you if you live in a rent-controlled area. I get it; you can only raise it a certain percentage per year. If you want to raise it because you're in a rent-controlled area, then weigh your options.

But if you're not in a rent-controlled area, do not raise your rent every year. When you raise your rent, you make your tenants think something like, *Bro, what the eff? I'll find a cheaper place to live!* And then they leave.

If you have a terrible tenant . . . well, maybe raising their rent is a tactic you'd like to try to get them to decide they'd like to try living in someone else's house. But, if you've found good tenants, avoid raising the rent for as long as possible. Trust me; a good, honest tenant is worth more than the extra $600 you'll get each year by raising the rent by $50 a month.

татк;DR

TL;DR

Your tenants will break things, make messes, and leave their stuff around the shared space. Accept it as one of the things you will need to deal with and move on. Do not try to be their mother (or father). As long as they aren't leaving crazy messes, destroying things, or letting dishes mold, it is probably something you can get past.

Get comfortable calling house meetings and addressing issues as they arise. Record the entire meeting or take notes and send your roommates those notes, especially if there are any action items or addendums to the rules.

Speaking of rules, having a rule book will save you a lot of back and forth because the expectations are written clearly. In addition to clear rules, a detailed contract will help you handle sticky issues most calmly and rationally. Be a house that runs based on *rules,* not *rulers.*

It may be a challenge to adjust to being a flatmate and a landlord; however, creating an environment of respect and protecting each other's boundaries will prevent major disagreements most of the time.

Conclusion

Action is a great restorer and builder of confidence. Inaction is not only the result, but the cause of fear.

— Norman Vincent Peale

I opened this book, as I always do, with a quote about creating wealth – *true* wealth, where you decide what you do with your time. House hacking could be the first step on a journey of thousands where *you* generate your true wealth.

Most Millennials believe that they will never own a house, which is usually the first step people take in creating wealth. It's baked into our culture: *houses are too expensive. I won't own one until I'm 50.* That's not true! And I hope this book has helped to show you that.

You need not wait until you're 50 to own a house. You can save up enough money to buy your own slightly oversized house and then rent out portions of it! And the neat part about that is if you are savvy with what house you buy, you can even repeat the process repeatedly until you've created a *House Hacking Empire*!

If you read this book solely to learn how to live for free, then I hope you got that – and more. This book was about far more than buying your own house, though you can just stop there if you'd like. This book was about creating passive income and working your way towards generational wealth.

I have helped so many others realize that they *can* own a house. They can do this! But they have to be smart about it. You can't waste your time on houses that don't work and tenants you don't like. This book contained all the usual tips and tricks I give my friends who have questions. The only thing I missed is a discussion about your budget, but you'll go through a mini-course on that if you subscribe to my newsletter, so be on the lookout!

The concept of house hacking is easy:

1. Buy a house with space you don't need
2. Rent out the rooms to people you like
3. ???
4. Prosper!

That's a little meme humor, for the uninitiated.

But the application of these concepts – actually *doing it*? That's scary. I hope this book has taken the edge off of some of your fear.

If you found this book helpful, I'd love to hear about it in the review section. If you enjoy my writing and want to know more about creating passive income, you can check out one of my other books, *No Property, No problem,* and *Beach House Business Model.*

No matter what your goals, I hope you blow past them. And I'm so honored that I get to be a part of it!

Cat

If you liked this book, please consider leaving a review. It helps the algorithm recommend our books to other FIRE hopefuls.

And don't forget to pick up your free goodies and join our newsletter at www.AutomatedRetirees.com/Live4Free!

And if you ever need help on your Fat FIRE journey, you can join our community at www.Facebook.com/groups/FatFired. We love helping our readers reach their FIRE goals and one of the best ways we can help do that is through our Facebook group.

See you there!

References

Quick Real Estate Statistics. (2020, November 11). National Association of Realtors. Retrieved March 3, 2020, from https://www.nar.realtor/research-and-statistics/quick-real-estate-statistics

7 Benefits of using proper management software. (n.d.). Headchannel.co.uk. Retrieved December 10, 2020, from https://headchannel.co.uk/7-benefits-of-using-property-management-software-321

Adams, K. (2020, October 29). *11 Mistakes inexperienced landlords make.* Investopedia. https://www.investopedia.com/financial-edge/0909/11-mistakes-inexperienced-landlords-make.aspx

Alesandra Dubin. (2020, January 24). *You could live in your house for free if you follow the rules of "House Hacking."* Good Housekeeping. https://www.goodhousekeeping.com/life/money/a30611975/what-is-house-hacking/#:~:text=That%20way%20the%20owners%20can

Black, K. (2019, December 2). *10 best landlord apps for 2019 / 20*. Landlord Insider. https://www.landlordvision.co.uk/blog/best-landlord-apps/

Davis, G. B. (2020, August 31). *House hacking: 10 Ways to live for free (Even in a single-family home)*. SparkRental. https://sparkrental.com/house-hacking-10-ways-live-for-free/

Fels, E. (2020, February 21). *5 Smart time management tips for small business Owners*. Business Know-How. https://www.businessknowhow.com/growth/time-management-tips.htm

Green. (2015, May 19). *8 House rules every landlord should explain to tenants*. Green Residential. https://www.greenresidential.com/8-house-rules-every-landlord-should-explain-to-tenants/

Greene, D. (2018, December 4). *House hacking: How financially savvy people live in expensive markets while saving money*. Forbes. https://www.forbes.com/sites/davidgreene/2018/12/04/house-hacking-how-financially-savvy-people-live-in-expensive-markets-while-saving-money/?sh=6b355d3570f0

Gregory, A. (2020, January 3). *7 Tips for More Effective Time Management.* The Balance Small Business. https://www.thebalancesmb.com/effective-time-management-tips-2951611

Grover, C. (2019). Oval mirror near toilet bowl. In *Pexels*. https://www.pexels.com/photo/oval-mirror-near-toilet-bowl-1910472/

Henry, D. (2020, March 24). *Passive income with benefits: House hacking.* Nomadic Real Estate. https://www.nomadicrealestate.com/passive-income-house-hacking/

Innago tenant and property management software - 2020 Pricing, features & demo. (n.d.). Www.Softwareadvice.com. Retrieved December 10, 2020, from https://www.softwareadvice.com/za/property/innago-profile/

Jankelow, L. (2020, September 30). *The secrets of writing rental listings.* Avail. https://www.avail.co/education/articles/secrets-of-writing-rental-listings

Living with a tenant - how to be a flatmate and a landlord at the same time. (2010, November 22). Century 21 Australia. https://www.century21.com.au/post/living-with-a-tenant-how-to-be-a-flatmate-and-a-landlord-at-the-same-time

Lopez, C. (2020, September 9). *Personal finances and goals for a house hack ⋆ Denver investment real estate.* Denver Investment Real Estate. https://www.denverinvestmentrealestate.com/personal-finances-and-goals-for-a-house-hack/

Mastroeni, T. (2020, June 24). *Your guide to long-distance real estate investing.* Millionacres. https://www.fool.com/millionacres/real-estate-investing/rental-properties/your-guide-to-long-distance-real-estate-investing/

Melnyczuk, T. (2020, November 26). *Photo by Tania Melnyczuk on Unsplash.* Unsplash.com. https://unsplash.com/photos/dSOQHP-ALqw

Ojeda, E. (2020, February 9). *How to automate your rental property.* Medium. https://medium.com/@ErnestoJOjeda/how-to-automate-your-rental-property-33d1e75a977b

PayProp software - 2020 Pricing, features & demo. (n.d.). Www.Softwareadvice.com. Retrieved December 10, 2020, from https://www.softwareadvice.com/za/property/payprop-profile/

Quicken software - 2020 Pricing, features & demo. (n.d.). Www.Softwareadvice.com. Retrieved December 10, 2020, from https://www.softwareadvice.com/za/property/quicken-profile/

Ratynski, A. (2020, September 22). *7 Practical tips for landlords dealing with terrible tenants.* Bay Property Management Group. https://www.baymgmtgroup.com/blog/7-actionable-tips-for-dealing-with-terrible-tenants/

Reed-Edens, K. (2016, January 22). *The TenantLoop App aims to improve landlord-renter communication (Finally!).* Entrepreneur Quarterly (EQ). https://entrepreneurquarterly.com/the-tenantloop-app-helps-landlords-and-renters-communicate-better/

RMH Editor. (2012, June 22). *rules for tenants | Renting My House: A guide for new landlords.*

Www.Rentingmyhouse.net. https://www.rentingmyhouse.net/tag/rules-for-tenants

Shalhout, S. (2020, July 22). *Long distance real estate investing: 7 mistakes you must avoid*. Investment Property Tips. https://www.mashvisor.com/blog/long-distance-real-estate-investing-mistakes/

Southworth, G. (n.d.). *How much should I charge to rent a room in my house?* Real Estate Info Guide. Retrieved December 7, 2020, from https://realestateinfoguide.com/how-much-should-i-charge-to-rent-a-room-in-my-house/

Top 25 websites for advertising your property rental listing. (2017, August 7). Propertyware. https://www.propertyware.com/blog/top-5-websites-for-advertising-your-property-rental-listing/

Tosolini, F. (2019, June 13). *White and beige marble-top table*. Unsplash.com. https://unsplash.com/photos/21xbUDIN8ao

Van Rensburg, D. J. (2019, October 19). *Pillows on bed*. Unsplash.com. https://unsplash.com/photos/_WEDFTZV0qU

Whitney, M. (2016). White bed comforter during bedtime. In *Pexels*. https://www.pexels.com/photo/white-bed-comforter-during-daytimne-90317/

www.ingramcontent.com/pod-product-compliance
Lightning Source LLC
Chambersburg PA
CBHW052357220526
45465CB00003BB/1141